T0329147

Cambridge Elements ≡

Elements in the Philosophy of Religion
edited by
Yujin Nagasawa
University of Birmingham

GOD AND EMOTION

R. T. Mullins
University of Edinburgh

CAMBRIDGE
UNIVERSITY PRESS

CAMBRIDGE
UNIVERSITY PRESS

University Printing House, Cambridge CB2 8BS, United Kingdom

One Liberty Plaza, 20th Floor, New York, NY 10006, USA

477 Williamstown Road, Port Melbourne, VIC 3207, Australia

314–321, 3rd Floor, Plot 3, Splendor Forum, Jasola District Centre,
New Delhi – 110025, India

79 Anson Road, #06–04/06, Singapore 079906

Cambridge University Press is part of the University of Cambridge.

It furthers the University's mission by disseminating knowledge in the pursuit of
education, learning, and research at the highest international levels of excellence.

www.cambridge.org
Information on this title: www.cambridge.org/9781108723411
DOI: 10.1017/9781108688918

© R. T. Mullins 2020

First published 2020

A catalogue record for this publication is available from the British Library.

ISBN 978-1-108-72341-1 Paperback
ISSN 2399-5165 (online)
ISSN 2515-9763 (print)

God and Emotion

Elements in the Philosophy of Religion

DOI: 10.1017/9781108688918
First published online: September 2020

R. T. Mullins
University of Edinburgh, Scotland
Author for correspondence: R. T. Mullins, rtmullins@gmail.com

Abstract: An introductory exploration on the nature of emotions, and examination of some of the critical issues surrounding the emotional life of God as they relate to happiness, empathy, love, and moral judgments. Covering the different criteria used in the debate between impassibility and passibility, readers can begin to think about which emotions can be predicated of God and which cannot.

Keywords: God, Emotion, Impassibility, Empathy

ISBNs: 9781108723411 (PB), 9781108688918 (OC)
ISSNs: 2399-5165 (online), 2515-9763 (print)

Contents

Introduction   1

1 Emotions   4

2 The Impassible God   15

3 The Passible God   25

4 The Love of God   34

5 The Wrath of God and Other Moral Judgments   50

6 Divine Empathy and the Problem of Creepy Emotions   60

Conclusion   69

Bibliography   70

Introduction

Many who affirm that God exists also believe that God is personal in some sense. Being personal is often associated with having a mental life that involves emotions. Does God have emotions? If so, which emotions does God have? As you are pondering these questions, consider how your answer makes you feel. Does the idea of an emotional God make you feel happy or sad? Do you feel comforted by the thought that God understands what it is like to be you? Perhaps you want a God who can say, "I feel your pain." Of course, the idea of an emotional God might disturb you. As you reflect on your own emotional state, or the emotional state of others, you might hope that no deity could be like that. Maybe instead, you are comforted by the thought that God is completely beyond all emotional states. These are interesting issues, and the history of philosophical theology is divided over how to think about them. Traditionally, these issues have centered on a debate between those who believe that God is impassible and those who believe that He is not.

During the patristic era of Christianity, the impassibility of God was held as an indisputable fact by orthodox and heretic alike. In part, the doctrine of divine impassibility teaches that God cannot suffer. As I shall explain later, various criteria were used to arrive at the conclusion that God cannot have the emotions associated with suffering. The assumption of impassibility played an influential role in shaping the early debates over the incarnation with positions being developed around ways to preserve the divine nature from suffering. Divine impassibility remained unquestioned throughout the Middle Ages, but received some scepticism during the Reformation and beyond. Yet the majority of Christians still affirmed that God cannot suffer.

Before the turn of the twentieth century, however, things began to change. A debate arose and the doctrine of impassibility underwent a newfound scrutiny. Various philosophers and theologians began to affirm the passibility, or suffering, of God with a greater fervour than before. In 1900, Marshall Randles commented that this modern rejection of divine impassibility is merely a passing mood that "will probably turn out to be one of those temporary reactions which come and go."[1] Given the long track record of divine impassibility, Randles' prediction would have seemed like a safe bet. However, the prediction turned out to be deeply mistaken. Far from a passing mood, the doctrine of divine passibility eventually came to be declared as the new orthodoxy within twentieth-century Christian theology. Various factors help explain this change of heart, but it is difficult to offer a full explanation of this new theological mood. For example, many theologians came to see divine impassibility as

---

[1] (Randles 1900, 5).

deeply unbiblical.[2] Others saw a conflict between impassibility and divine love because divine empathy became a hallmark for understanding God's love.[3] This is quite different from the traditional impassibilist view, which explicitly denies that God has empathy.[4]

One interesting feature about the affirmation of divine passibility in twentieth-century theology is that it serves as a common ground between seemingly diverse theological systems. Divine suffering is affirmed in process theism, liberation theology, ecofeminism, open theism, and beyond. One can even find Calvinists and Arminians affirming divine passibility. Groups of theologians who can often find little to agree on can all share their love of the suffering God. Truly, we live in a golden age of divine suffering.

However, not all are able to rejoice in an age of divine suffering. Indeed, one might think that such an age is something to be lamented. In spite of the apparent orthodoxy of divine passibility today, the doctrine of divine impassibility continues to have support from theologians and philosophers.[5] In fact, I would hazard a prediction that divine impassibility is going to make a comeback in twenty-first-century philosophical theology. If I, like Randles, am deeply mistaken in this prediction, we can both have a laugh over this in heaven.

For many, the debate between divine impassibility and divine passibility will seem extremely puzzling. The arguments for either view can sometimes be difficult to untangle, and the rhetoric from both sides can seem uncharitable at times. Passibilists will accuse the impassible God of being apathetic. Impassibilists will assert that the passible God is a creature or an idol. With rhetoric like this, one might think that we are living in a golden age of theological suffering. To make matters even more complicated, some contemporary theologians try to claim that God is both impassible and passible.[6] How is one supposed to make sense of all of this? I strongly suspect that there is a lack of understanding in the contemporary world of philosophical theology as to what the doctrine of impassibility actually affirms. At times, it seems as if contemporary thinkers are simply talking past one another because they are focusing on different kinds of issue.

In contemporary discussions of the doctrine of divine impassibility, different groups focus on different questions. As Anastasia Scrutton points out, contemporary theologians primarily focus on the question, "Can God Suffer?" whereas contemporary philosophers of religion focus on the question, "Does God have emotions?"[7] I believe that these questions are fundamentally related, but the

---

[2] Cf. (Bauckham 2008) (Moltmann 2001) (Fretheim 1984).   [3] (Herdt 2001, 369).

[4] (Davies 2006, 234).   [5] (Dolezal 2019).

[6] (Lister 2013) Cf. (Helm 2014, 151–3) for criticism of Lister.   [7] (Scrutton 2013, 866).

way the debates have unfolded has sometimes missed these connections. This is partly due to the fact that contemporary critics of impassibility sometimes caricature the impassible God as lacking all emotion. As one shall see in Section 2, the impassible God does have emotions, and these emotions explain why God cannot suffer. Thus, the issue is not *if* God has emotions. The real debate between impassibility and passibility is over which emotions God *can* have.

In this Element, I shall offer an introductory exploration on the nature of emotions, and examine some of the critical issues surrounding the emotional life of God as they relate to happiness, empathy, love, and moral judgments. I shall introduce the different criteria that are used in the debate between impassibility and passibility to help readers begin to think about which emotions can be predicated of God and which cannot.

In Section 1, I shall introduce some relevant issues within the philosophy of emotion. In Section 2, I shall locate the doctrine of divine impassibility within classical theism. This section will look at the classical criteria for discerning which emotions can literally be predicated of God.[8] Then I will argue that the classical understanding of God's happiness explains why the impassible God cannot suffer. In Section 3, I shall turn my attention to the doctrine of divine passibility. Given the diversity of theological positions that affirm passibility, I shall narrow my focus on a model of God called neoclassical theism.[9] It will be shown which criteria the passibilist affirms for discerning which emotions can literally be predicated of God. I will argue that the passibilist's understanding of God's omnisubjectivity, or maximal empathy, explains why the passible God can suffer.

With these positions demarcated, I will examine arguments for and against impassibility and passibility. These arguments will tease out various issues surrounding the nature of emotions and God's emotional life. Section 4 will consider the issue of God's love, and whether or not God's love is responsive to the value of creation. It will be shown that the impassible God's love is completely uninfluenced by the value of anything external to God, whereas the passible God's love is responsive to the value of creation. Based on this, passibilists often argue that the impassible God cannot genuinely love His creatures. Classical theists typically reject these arguments because they affirm

---

[8] It should be noted that both analogical and univocal predications of God are literal. Cf. (Muis 2011).

[9] The term "neoclassical theism" was once used to describe process theism before process theism became a well-established model of God. Following contemporary taxonomies for models of God in (Diller and Kasher 2013), neoclassical theism is now considered a distinct model from process theism. The details of neoclassical theism will be discussed in Section 3.

a different understanding of divine love from their passibilist interlocutors. I will consider a new argument that seeks to show an inconsistency between impassibility and the classical theist's own understanding of divine love. I will argue that divine passibility can better satisfy the classical understanding of divine love.

In Section 5, I will turn my attention towards God's evaluative moral judgments. I will argue that there is an incoherence between divine wrath and impassibility. I will also consider objections to the passible God's evaluative judgments. Some have argued that a passible God's emotions are so unstable that God cannot make sound moral judgments, or issue trustworthy promises about future salvation.

In Section 6, I shall consider objections to divine passibility based on moral problems for divine empathy. Some have argued that an empathetic God would have immoral emotions. I shall examine two possible ways for the passibilist to respond to this objection.

Given the short, introductory nature of this Element, I will not claim to have made a decisive case for either position. My aim here is merely to introduce readers to some of the complicated problems surrounding the topic of God and emotion. My hope is that by untangling these issues, and laying the problems bare before the reader's eyes, progress will become possible in the debate over God's emotional life.

1 Emotions

In this first section, I shall introduce some basic concepts within the philosophy of emotion. In particular, I shall discuss the cognitive and affective nature of emotions, and the relationship between emotions, truth, and morality.

§1.1 More Than a Feeling

What is an emotion? An emotion is a mental state that involves an evaluation that has a positive or negative affect. This implies that an emotion has two features: a cognitive component and an affective component. The cognitive component is what the emotion is about. The affective component is what the emotion *feels* like.

This might sound like an odd definition of an emotion, but its roots go all the way back to the Stoics in ancient Greece, and it still has many able defenders to this day. Of course, one might complain that this definition of an emotion is too cold, too clinical, perhaps too Stoic, to capture what an emotion really is.

Most of us today are not ancient Stoics. When a contemporary person is asked to think about emotions, what will most likely come to mind are feelings.

However, a Stoic philosopher might ask us to calm down and consider the Stoic definition for a moment. The philosopher will agree that feelings are an important constituent of an emotion. She will remind you that the definition of an emotion given above includes an affective component. An affect of an emotion is the way an emotion feels, and the feeling has a valence of positive or negative, or pleasant or unpleasant. Yet the philosopher will go on to say that feelings are not enough to capture what an emotion is. This is because there are several different kinds of phenomenon that involve feelings, like bodily sensations, and not all these feelings are emotions. As we shall see in Section 2, proponents of impassibility will even say that some emotions need not involve any bodily sensations at all. For the moment, however, a Stoic philosopher is merely wishing to say that there is a distinction between emotions and all the things that we typically associate with feelings. She will say that more is needed than mere feelings in order to distinguish emotions from these other phenomena.

Consider the statement, "Sally is cold." There are several ways to interpret this. In one interpretation, "Sally is cold" is a description of Sally's body temperature. In another, "Sally is cold" is a description of Sally's emotional life. Both interpretations involve feelings. The temperature of Sally's body certainly feels a particular way, but nothing about the feeling of being cold obviously implies anything about Sally's emotional life. According to the philosopher, in order to accurately describe Sally's emotional life, one will need to appeal to more than mere feelings.

Many philosophers contend that emotions cannot be mere feelings because emotions have a cognitive component as well as the affective component. To say that emotions are cognitive means that emotions have a representational content about the world. When one is having an emotion, one is seeing the world as being a certain way. Emotions involve evaluations about something in the world, and the content of that evaluation often makes one feel a particular way.[10]

What distinguishes emotions from bodily sensations is that emotions are always about something. Emotions always have some object or situation that they aim to evaluative and represent.[11] As Martha C. Nussbaum explains:

> If we really were to think of emotions as like bodily tugs or stabs or flashes, then we would precisely leave out what is most disturbing about them. How simple life would be, if grief were only a pain in the leg, or jealousy but a very bad backache. Jealousy and grief torment us mentally; it is the thoughts we have about objects that are the source of agony – and, in other cases, delight.[12]

---

[10] (Roberts 2013, 114–15). [11] (Deonna and Teroni 2012, 3–6). [12] (Nussbaum 2001, 16).

For philosophers such as Nussbaum, emotions have cognitive and affective features. The cognitive feature of emotions is what makes emotions unique from other affective phenomena, including bodily sensations. For instance, having a stubbed toe involves the feeling or affect of pain, but the pain of a stubbed toe is not an emotion. The pain of a stubbed toe will most likely cause one to have an emotion, but the emotions it can cause will be varied. One might become angry at the table for always being in the way. Or one might become annoyed at oneself for not turning the light on before walking down a dark hallway in the middle of the night. Yet, notice that the bodily sensation of pain is not an emotion. The pain of the stubbed toe has no cognitive content. It is not about anything, it is simply pain. Whereas the emotion of anger is about something. When angry, one judges that the table is an appropriate object of one's wrath. This judgment might involve describing the table with all sorts of colorful evaluative terms.

If you are feeling confused by this distinction between the cognitive and affective features of emotions, notice that you are judging this to be a confusing idea. Further, notice that there is a way that it feels to be confused. Hopefully, this confusion has turned into curiosity, and you feel motivated to investigate the cognitive nature of emotions further.

§1.2 The Cognitive Nature of Emotions

One of the interesting developments in contemporary studies of emotion is the focus on the cognitive nature of emotions. To help one understand the cognitive nature of emotions, philosophers will sometimes say that emotions are something akin to perception. When a person perceives something, she is seeing or construing the world to be a certain way.[13] Her perception is a kind of responsiveness to the object of her perception. Emotions are like this, too. Emotions involve a kind of responsiveness to the world where one construes the object of the emotion as being a certain way, such as *good, bad, fearsome, hopeful*, or *exciting*. For example, one might construe a barking dog as dangerous, and thus judge the dog a thing to be feared.

There are more similarities between perceptions and emotions that are worth considering. Perceptions are subject to standards of correctness depending on how well the construal tracks reality. If a person's construal of the object fails to properly represent the object, her perception will need to be corrected. The same can be said of emotions. If an emotion fails to construe an object or situation a certain way, it will be subject to correction.[14]

---

[13] (Roberts 2013, 46).   [14] (Helm 2015, 417–18).

Perhaps an illustration will help. Imagine that Sally walks into her living room and perceives that her pet cat is sitting on the mat. Her perception is responsive to a particular object – the cat on the mat. Her perception involves her immediately forming the belief, "The cat is on the mat." Her belief is correct insofar as there is a cat sitting on the mat. If there is no cat on the mat, her perception has misled her, and she will need to correct her belief.

Now imagine that Sally has a son named Ben who likes to play practical jokes. Ben has found a toy cat that has an uncanny resemblance to the family pet. Unbeknownst to Sally, Ben has placed the toy cat on the mat. When Sally walks in the room, she sees the cat and forms the belief, "The cat is on the mat." She calls the cat over so that she can pet it, but the cat does not move. She then hears Ben giggling. At first, Sally is confused, but then investigates further. She soon discovers Ben's clever ruse, and forms the belief, "The cat is not on the mat. That is a toy cat." In this instance, Sally no longer accepts what she perceived to be the case. She saw the world to be a certain way, but has come to reject the perception as a mere appearance that fails to track reality.

The claim from various philosophers of emotion is that emotions are similar to perceptions in that emotions involve a kind of representation of the world that is subject to correction depending on how well the emotion tracks reality. However, there are differences between emotions and perceptions that are salient to the discussion of this Element. Perceptions and emotions both give one a kind of experiential acquaintance with the object being perceived, but emotions are not mere perceptions. With perceptions, one has a direct access to the objects in the world, and this access need not be mediated by any other mental states. Emotions, however, are always grounded in some other mental states that are about the object of the emotion. These other mental states serve as the cognitive basis for the emotion.[15]

Some philosophers claim that the cognitive basis for emotions involves what one cares about or is concerned with.[16] Hence, emotions are not merely perceptions or ways of construing the world. Instead, emotions are *concern-based* construals that involve evaluative judgments about the objects being perceived. Unlike emotions, a perception need not involve any kind of evaluation of what is being perceived, whereas an emotion involves an evaluation of what is being perceived. This might sound somewhat technical, so I shall explain a little more what evaluations and concern-based construals are.

What does it mean to say that emotions are evaluative? To say that an emotion is evaluative is to say that one believes that the object of her emotion has certain kinds of value or axiological properties.[17] An object or circumstance has value

---

[15] (Deonna and Teroni 2012, 5).   [16] (Roberts 2007, 15).   [17] (Todd 2014, 706).

to an agent if she perceives or judges it to be worthy of her attention, and worthy of her to act on behalf of. In making this evaluation, she perceives an object or circumstance to have certain values, for example, *good, bad, fearsome, hopeful,* or *exciting*. Depending on which values she judges the circumstance to have, she will act differently. For example, if a person judges a barking dog to be fearsome, she might respond by running away. She deems the barking dog to be worth paying attention to, and worth responding to.

What does it mean to say that emotions are concern-based construals? In order to better understand this claim, it is worth emphasizing that emotions always have what we care about or value in the background. These cares and concerns are shaped by our beliefs, our desires to see the world change in a particular way, and the different narratives that make up our psychological identity. For example, the concerns of a devout Jew will be shaped by the narrative of Moses. The concerns of a devout Christian will be shaped by Moses, but will be more deeply influenced by the narrative of Jesus. The concerns of a Wall Street stockbroker will most likely be different from the concerns of a Marxist given the kind of economic policies each one affirms. These different kinds of concern make up one's cognitive basis.

The cognitive basis of what one cares about creates a disposition to have certain kinds of emotional responses or evaluative judgments about objects or circumstances in the world. If you don't care about something, you are not disposed to pay attention to it, neither are you motivated to act on its behalf.[18] If you do care about something, you will be disposed to pay attention to it, and you will be motivated to act on its behalf.

There are different ways that philosophers speak of these dispositions.[19] Sometimes these dispositions are referred to as a person's sentiments, and other times the dispositions are taken to be part of a person's moral character. A moral character trait is a disposition towards certain virtues or vices. For example, a person might have the character trait of *kindness* or *cruelty*. A kind person is one who is disposed to act in kind ways, whereas a cruel person is one who is disposed to act in cruel ways. A sentiment is similar, but involves a disposition towards a specific thing like a person, an animal, or an institution. Love and hate are classic examples of sentiments. Two lovers are disposed to act in loving ways towards one another, whereas two enemies are disposed to act in hateful ways towards one another.[20]

It is important to distinguish between the disposition to have an emotion, and actually having an emotion. One might be disposed to be angry with an annoying neighbor, but that is different from actually being angry with the

---

[18] (Helm 2015, 429).   [19] Cf. (Heil 2018).   [20] (Deonna and Teroni 2012, 108–9).

neighbor. An emotion is a mental state that involves the evaluation or concern-based construal, and involves a positive or negative affect.[21] The emotion is a manifestation of the disposition that makes up one's cognitive basis.

As a way to tease out these notions, let's consider Sally again. For as long as you have known Sally, it has been clear that she cares deeply about her grandmother. In other words, Sally has certain sentiments or dispositions towards her grandmother. Imagine that Sally has received a phone call. The person on the phone is a nurse informing Sally that she has lost her grandmother to dementia. Sally experiences sorrow over hearing of the loss of her grandmother. Her sentiments towards her grandmother find expression in the emotion of grief. That seems like an appropriate response to the situation. Sally is recalling the great value of her grandmother, and is upset by perceiving the great disvalue of losing her grandmother. Sally's attention is on the loss of her grandmother, and Sally's tears are the fitting action. In that moment, nothing else around Sally grabs her attention. Her attention is focused on the news about her grandmother. One might say that Sally's sadness tracks the values of the circumstances.

§1.3 Emotions and Truth

All of this talk about tracking values naturally raises an important question for our discussion. Can emotions be true or false, rational or irrational? Sometimes people feel uncomfortable with this question. Sometimes different voices in our contemporary culture say that it is unacceptable to tell someone else how to feel, or that one cannot tell a person that her emotions are wrong. Yet, one will often hear that she should be outraged by the most recent political event. She might even notice that people will give her judgmental looks if she does not share their outrage. This should push us to consider the relationship between emotions, truth, and rationality a bit further.

Consider some more mundane expression that you often hear such as, "You are overreacting," or, "There is no use in crying over spilt milk." Perhaps you have said something like, "There is no reason to feel bad about what happened. You did the right thing." These common examples seem to presuppose that emotions can be subject to some sort of standard of correctness. These examples assume that there is a way that an emotion should correspond to reality, thus suggesting that the emotions can be rational or irrational, or true or false, depending on how well they track the values in reality, and how well in line they are with one's pattern of commitments and considered judgments.[22]

---

[21] Cf. (Soteriou 2018).   [22] (Helm 2001, 195).

Julien A. Deonna and Fabrice Teroni point out that there are different standards by which one assesses emotions in terms of an emotion's correctness and justification.[23] Consider first the standard of correctness. As stated before, emotions are cognitive in that they represent the world as being a certain way. An emotion construes objects in the world as having certain values or axiological properties. The standard of correctness assesses an emotion's truth value. An emotion is true or false depending on if it accurately represents the values present in the world.[24] Imagine that Sally is watching a sad movie. Sally's emotion of sadness towards the movie is true if and only if the movie is sad.

Another standard for assessing an emotion is justification. An emotion is justified if one has good reasons for evaluating an object to have certain values, and if she lacks any defeaters for her initial evaluation. Often times, in the absence of defeaters, the emotional experience itself will be the justifying reason for her evaluation. Emotional experiences give a person an initial evaluation of a situation, and these evaluations serve as the basis for our considered judgments. If a person's cognitive faculties are functioning properly, she will often be warranted in accepting the evaluations of her emotions. Again, if Sally sees a sad movie and starts to cry, one might say that Sally's emotion of sadness is warranted because any fairly normal person who sees that movie would feel sad.

Of course, people often feel the need to question their emotions. As Michael S. Brady points out, there are many situations in which a person will feel compelled to seek out further justification for her judgment instead of simply accepting the evaluation of her emotion.[25] On hearing a strange noise at night, one might initially feel scared, but then question her own fear. She might think, "There is no reason to be scared. It is probably nothing. Surely it is not a scary monster … no, no, no. It is nothing. Just the wind!" Yet, notice that I said one will *feel compelled* to seek out further justification for her judgment. This is because it is one's emotions that motivate her to seek further reasons to accept or reject her initial evaluation. So not only can emotions be justified by reasons, but emotions also facilitate the search for justifying reasons by focusing one's attention on the object of our emotional experience for further consideration.[26]

The relationship between emotions, truth, and justification is what helps distinguish emotions from other affective states such as moods. Moods have an affect in the same way that emotions do, but moods do not have a representational content or any obvious connection to truth. With emotions one can ask

---

[23] (Deonna and Teroni 2012, 7).   [24] (Roberts 2013, 91).   [25] (Brady 2013, 86–90).
[26] (Brady 2013, 93)

questions such as "why are you sad today?," or "what made you so happy?" Emotions are subject to these kinds of question because emotions are about particular objects or situations in the world. Moods, however, are not about any particular object or situation. When one is in a mood, grumpiness say, this mood is not directed at any particular object or situation. Instead, one is in a general state of grumpiness towards everything.

Since moods are not directed at any particular object or situation, they nonrationally influence the way one responds to the world. A grumpy person is disposed to see just about everything as terrible regardless of what values are in a given circumstance. The kind of emotions, or evaluative judgments, that grumpiness gives rise to will be mostly negative. This is why some philosophers say that if an emotion is based on a mood, the justification for the emotion will be called into question. Moods are often used to excuse certain kinds of emotion, but they are not used to *justify* an emotion.[27]

Consider Sally again. Sally has been going through a difficult time at work, and she is feeling angry with her boss. Say that Sally is asked why she is angry with her boss. If her response is, "I was in a bad mood," one will most likely not see her anger as justified. But imagine she offers a different reply. Sally tells you about the way her boss has been treating her, and it sounds deeply unfair. You then find yourself uttering these words: "You have every right to be angry. You have been treated unfairly." What you seem to be saying is that Sally's emotion of anger is justified because it is a fitting response to her situation. Her emotion has correctly construed the evaluative property in this scenario, that of *being unfair*.

However, there is more to the story of emotions, truth, and justification. One must also consider how proportionate the emotional response is to the situation. It is not enough to correctly identify the values in a given situation, and have good reasons for this judgment. One must also capture the right degree of intensity of the value in a given situation. If an emotional response fails to properly track the value of the object, the emotional response is not rational. If an emotional response properly tracks the value of the object, the emotional response is rational.[28]

Return to Sally. It might be the case that Sally has correctly identified her situation as being unfair, but that does not necessarily mean that she has captured the right intensity of the unfairness. Imagine that Sally's situation involves a mild offense. Perhaps her boss miscalculated her working hours, and accidentally failed to pay Sally for an hour's worth of work. Further, assume that this is a one-off incident, and not a recurring pattern of behavior from her

[27] (Deonna and Teroni 2012, 105–6).   [28] (Todd 2014, 704).

boss. Surely, in this situation Sally is justified in being angry because she has been treated unfairly. However, it would not seem rational for Sally to start baying for her boss's blood. The demand for blood seems deeply disproportionate to the degree of unfairness in Sally's situation. Instead, it would seem more rational for Sally to inform her boss of the miscalculation, and to demand proper compensation for her work.

§1.4 Emotions and Morality

There is more to the story of emotions that is worth considering for the discussion of this Element. Since emotions involve evaluations, there is a close connection between emotions and morality. In fact, some philosophers say that emotions are what enable us to apprehend or consciously grasp the values in the world.[29]

There are several kinds of relationship between emotions and morality, but space limitations allow me to focus on only a few. First, however, I need to make a stipulation about morality. There are various debates within moral philosophy over whether or not morality is purely subjective, or if there are objective moral facts and values. Personally, I affirm a view known as moral realism, which says that there are objective, mind-independent moral facts and values that exist in the world.[30] I shall assume this position since most theists affirm moral realism, or something quite like it. Further, one can argue that it makes no sense to talk of emotions being subject to standards of correctness and justification if there are no objective values in the world. Part of what it means for an emotion to be appropriate or reasonable is for the emotion to justifiedly represent an object as having certain values.[31] With this stipulation in place, I wish to note that there are objective and subjective values.

Objective values are the evaluative properties that things have regardless of whether or not someone recognizes them. For example, theists claim that God is objectively the most valuable being in the world because God is the greatest good. Subjective values are the patterns of commitments and judgments that a person has. A person's subjective values may or may not line up with the objective values that exist in the world. For instance, a theist will insist that a person should acknowledge the objective value of God, and prioritize her commitments accordingly. A theist might complain that a particular person's judgments about the value of God are mistaken if that person does not perceive how great God is. With this in mind, allow me to tease out these ideas by considering five different issues about emotions and values.

---

[29] (Roberts 2013, 115).   [30] (Shafer-Landau 2005) (Cuneo 2007).
[31] (Deonna and Teroni 2012, 41–9).

First, emotions can reveal what a person subjectively values. Again, emotions involve evaluations grounded in what a person cares about. When you consider a person's pattern of commitments and judgments, you can discern what that person really values.[32] On seeing Sally's sadness at the news of her grandmother, one can see that her sadness reveals how much she cares about her grandmother. Sally's emotions reveal her subjective values.

Second, emotions can be revelatory of objective value. Emotions can give a person an experiential acquaintance with the value of an object. A person might theoretically know that God is good, but have little concern about the divine. A theist will insist that this is not enough to really understand God's goodness. Instead, she will say that a person must come to know how good God is by experiencing the goodness of God. Through a direct, experiential acquaintance with God, a person will come to know the value of God in a profoundly new way.[33] The seventeenth-century preacher Rev. William Bates explains that when a person understands an object as worthy, her will and affections are inclined towards the object. Thus, Bates says, when a person discovers "the transcendent excellencies [sic] in God, the soul is excited to love and to delight in him as its supreme good, it is then really and perfectly happy."[34]

However, I must emphasize that emotions *can* be revelatory of objective value, but they might not. This is because emotions are evaluations about what one takes to be worthy of her attention and action based on background concerns. Theists have long insisted that one's emotional states and prior concerns can prevent one from properly perceiving the objective values in the world because a person's subjective judgments about what is worthy of her attention can fail to correspond to the objective values in the world. If a person does not have her emotions properly attuned to the world, she might miss out on certain things. For instance, a person might not be able to understand the concept of benevolence because she is not herself benevolent. Hence, theists have often claimed that a person must train her passionate reasoning and judgments in such a way that she is better primed to respond to the objective values in the world. This might involve cultivating certain virtuous traits such as a desire to search for truth, beauty, and goodness. Yet some theists think this is not enough. Some theists claim that God needs to give humans a special act of grace that enables humans to develop the right affections towards God and the universe. Otherwise, humans will never have the right affections to properly know God.[35]

---

[32] (Scrutton 2011, 72). [33] (Scrutton 2011, 70–1). [34] (Bates 1999, 188).
[35] (Wainwright 2016, 61).

Third, emotions motivate moral reasoning. Again, emotions are evaluations of what one takes to be worthy of attention. Robert C. Roberts notes several ways in which emotions can support moral reasoning. For example, our emotions are often the starting points for our moral reasoning. Emotions produce the moral premises that we reason about. Our emotions keep our attention locked in on the object of our moral deliberation because we judge the object of our emotion to be worthy of our attention.[36]

Fourth, emotions motivate moral action. What I have in mind here is not how the affect or feelings of an emotion motivate action. It is true that the affect of an emotion can often motivate our actions. We can easily have our heartstrings plucked to get us to do things. Yet various philosophers maintain that this is not the only way in which emotions explain moral actions. It is the cognitive component of emotions that does most of the explanatory work. Emotions are evaluations of what one takes to be worthy of action.[37] When a person perceives the value of an object, she is motivated to act. Without the evaluation, it is difficult to discern why a person acts as she does. In fact, some philosophers say that just to have an emotion is to be moved to action.[38] A person acts on behalf of something precisely because she judges it to have some kind of value.

The Christian tradition has long acknowledged the role that emotions play in motivating moral action. Early Christian sermons would draw people's attention to the suffering of others, and ask the audience to engage in empathy with the plight of others. Through empathy, the preacher would focus the audience's attention to the value of those in need. Those in need are made in the image of God just like you and I are. Through empathy, the preacher would attempt to motivate the audience to act on behalf of those in need.[39]

Fifth, emotions can be subject to moral correction. Earlier, I noted that an emotion can be true or false depending on how well the emotion represents reality. This claim about moral correction is one step further. A person's emotions have an evaluative content that reveals what she subjectively cares about. What a person subjectively cares about can be corrected depending on how well her concern-based construals of reality actually match moral reality. The way this correction is understood will depend on one's ethical theory, or one's moral framework. It will also be understood as relative to the individual's network of prior experiences, commitments, and obligations.

Consider an example from virtue theory, which says that a virtuous person has the right kinds of affective disposition. Her moral character is such that she is disposed to have the most fitting kinds of emotional response to the world

---

[36] (Roberts 2013, 61–6). Cf. (Clore 2011).   [37] (Roberts 2013, 115–21).
[38] (Helm 2001, 193–9).   [39] Cf. (Wessel 2016).

around her. For example, Thomas Aquinas says that a virtuous person will be disturbed by witnessing a horrendous event. Perhaps a person feels sorrow over the event. Her sorrow will reveal that she has perceived evil in the event. Aquinas says that her sorrow also reveals that she rejects the evil she has perceived. But what if a person is not disturbed by the evil in the event? If a person is not disturbed, this will reveal several possible things about the person. Perhaps she is ignorant of what evil is, and thus is unable to recognize the evil contained in the event. Alternatively, her lack of sorrow could reveal that she does not reject the evil, or that she is ambivalent towards the evil she has witnessed.[40] As such, she will need to have more training in virtue because her moral and emotional character is not attuned to reality.

Interestingly, Aquinas also affirms that the impassible God is never disturbed by anything. So one may wonder if the impassible God is truly virtuous.[41] However, that is a conversation for another day.

Conclusion

With the discussion on the nature of emotions behind us, I can now turn to consider the emotional life of God. As stated before, theists of different persuasions will differ on which emotions can be predicated of God. In the next two sections, I will seek to uncover the rationality behind these differences in order to identify the underlying criteria that one can use to discern exactly which emotions can be predicated of God.

2 The Impassible God

In the introduction to this Element, I noted that the traditional view among Christian theists is that God is impassible. I identified different kinds of question that contemporary theologians and philosophers of religion ask about God with regards to the doctrine of divine impassibility. Theologians typically ask "Can God suffer?," whereas philosophers of religion ask "Can God have emotions?" In this section, I shall argue that the impassible God does have emotions, and that these emotions explain why the impassible God cannot suffer. This is because impassibility is best understood within the context of classical theism, and classical theism contains certain criteria for discerning which emotions can be predicated of God.

§2.1 Locating Impassibility Within Classical Theism

The doctrine of divine impassibility is best understood within the classical conception of God, which includes attributes such as timelessness, immutability,

---

[40] (Aquinas, *Summa Theologiae* 2.Q39.a2).   [41] (Wolterstorff 2010, 223–38).

and simplicity. To be sure, classical theism also affirms attributes such as aseity, self-sufficiency, omnipotence, omniscience, and so on, but such attributes are also affirmed by theists who endorse divine passibility. What makes classical theism unique is its commitment to divine timelessness, immutability, simplicity, and impassibility since these attributes are held to be systematically connected. It must also be understood that classical theism affirms certain principles, assumptions, and divine attributes that other theists will deny. Since I have articulated and explored some of these issues elsewhere, I shall here seek to offer a brief discussion of the classical attributes to help set the stage for understanding divine impassibility.[42] This will also help one understand what divine passibility is affirming and rejecting.

To begin our discussion, allow me to make a few quick remarks about the nature of time. Classical theists have historically affirmed a relational theory of time, and a presentist ontology of time. On a relational theory of time, time exists if and only if a change occurs. This is because a change creates a before and an after, and part of the nature of time involves events being in before and after relations. On presentism, only the present moment of time exists. Past moments of time no longer exist, and future moments of time do not yet exist. The present exhausts all reality. Hence, whatever exists exists at the present.[43]

Classical theism used these assumptions about the nature of time to articulate divine timelessness. On classical theism, one of the key characteristics of a temporal object is that it undergoes change and succession. One of the key characteristics of a timeless being is that it does not undergo change or succession. To say that God is timeless is to say that God's life lacks a beginning, an end, and succession. A timeless God dwells in an eternal present that lacks a before and after.[44]

Why does the timeless God dwell in an eternal present that lacks a before and after? This is because a timeless God is also an immutable God. An immutable God cannot change in any way, shape, or form. Since part of the nature of time involves undergoing change, an immutable God is said to be void of all temporality because He is void of all change. On the classical understanding of immutability, God cannot undergo any intrinsic or any extrinsic changes.[45] Any intrinsic or extrinsic change would render God mutable and temporal.[46] Hence, classical theism denies all change of God.

---

[42] (Mullins 2016a).

[43] Some contemporary classical theists affirm an eternalist ontology of time. On eternalism, all moments of time exist. For discussion, see (Mullins 2016a) chapter 6.

[44] (Strong 1907a, 275).   [45] (Lombard, *Sentences* I, Distinction XXXVII.7).

[46] (Helm 2010, 19–20, 81–6) (Deng 2018, 36).

With these brief statements on timelessness and immutability, we can move on to divine simplicity. On the classical understanding of God, all God's essential attributes are both identical to one another, and identical to God's nature and existence. For example, God's attribute of omniscience is identical to God's omnipotence, and these, in turn, are identical to God's nature and existence. With creatures like you and me, we are substances that possess properties such as knowledge and power. With the simple God, this is not the case. The simple God does not possess any properties. Instead, there is the simple, undivided substance that we call God. This simple substance does not have any intrinsic or extrinsic properties because it does not possess any properties at all.[47] As Peter Lombard makes clear: "The same substance alone is properly and truly simple in which there is no diversity or change or multiplicity of parts, or accidents, or of any other forms."[48]

Further, a simple God is purely actual. This means that the simple God does not possess any potential whatsoever. On classical theism, it is assumed that to possess potentiality implies mutability since going from potential to actual entails undergoing a change. Classical theism has already ruled out any kind of change in God, so a simple God must be purely actual. The claim that God is pure actuality and simple has further entailments. It entails that all of God's actions are identical to one another such that there is only one divine act. Further, this one divine act is identical to the divine substance.[49]

Earlier I noted that classical theists and nonclassical theists agree that God is omniscient. However, there are differences over the nature and extent of omniscience that are relevant to understanding the emotional life of God. On classical theism, God is said to know the truth values of all propositions by having a perfect introspective knowledge of Himself. God's knowledge is in no way based on a perception of the universe. The classical theist would consider perceptual knowledge a deficiency because it would make God's knowledge dependent on creation.[50] Instead, classical theists affirm that God knows the truth values of all propositions through a single, introspective act.[51]

This raises a particular problem for classical theism because some propositions change their truth values over time. Tenseless propositions do not change their truth value over time, whereas tensed propositions do. This is because tensed propositions contain references to the past, present, or future, thus making their truth value dependent on what time it is now. Tenseless propositions specify a precise time without reference to the past, present, or future thus

---

[47] (Augustine, *The Trinity* VII.10.) (Rogers 1996, 166).
[48] (Lombard, *Sentences* I, Dist. VIII.3).   [49] (Aquinas, *Summa Contra Gentiles* II.10).
[50] (Augustine, *The Trinity* XV.13.22).   [51] (Charnock 1864, 464ff).

making their truth value independent of what time it is now.[52] An example of a tenseless proposition is <Sally sits on top of Arthur's Seat at 2:00pm on April 4, 2019>. If this proposition is true, it is always true. Nothing about what time it is now changes the truth value of this proposition. An example of a tensed proposition is <Sally is now sitting on top of Arthur's Seat>. This proposition changes its truth value depending on what time it is now, or how the world is at present.

A common point of contention over classical theism is how a timeless God can know the truth values of tensed propositions. If God knows the truth values of tensed propositions, God's knowledge would change over time, thus violating timelessness and immutability. The traditional classical theist response is to say that God does not know the truth values of tensed propositions because such knowledge would make God dependent on creation. The classical theist sees this dependency as an imperfection, and so excludes this kind of knowledge from God.[53] As I shall discuss in the next section, the passibilist does not see this kind of dependency as a problem, and will claim that the passible God knows more than the classical God.

All of this talk about dependency brings up two further attributes that are worth discussing for the purposes of this Element: aseity and self-sufficiency. One might wonder why I have withheld a discussion of these attributes until now. Classical theists often claim that God's aseity and self-sufficiency entail that God is timeless, immutable, simple, and impassible. As I have argued elsewhere, I cannot find any such systematic entailment from aseity and self-sufficiency to divine timelessness, immutability, simplicity, and impassibility. Yet, classical theists insist that these attributes play such a role.[54] Instead, it seems to me that classical theists are sneaking in attributes such as divine simplicity into their definitions of aseity and self-sufficiency.[55] This being the case, it is important to define these attributes clearly.

Divine aseity is a claim about God's self-existence or independent existence. Aseity is affirming that God's existence is not derived from anything else. It can be stated as follows:

> Aseity: A being exists *a se* if and only if its existence is in no way dependent on, or derived from, anything external.

If that is aseity, one will rightly ask what self-sufficiency is. As the seventeenth-century theologian Christopher Blackwood explains, God's self-sufficiency is an attribute of God's perfect nature. Self-sufficiency expresses

---

[52] Of course, this account of propositions depends on various commitments one has within the philosophy of time, semantics, and truthmaker theory.
[53] (Mullins, 2016, chapter 4).   [54] (Dolezal 2019, 17–23).   [55] (Mullins 2018).

the fact that God has all the perfections that we find in creatures. His possession of these perfections is not dependent on anything outside of Himself. God has no need for anything outside Himself in order to be perfect. In fact, God is the cause and source of all the perfections we find in creation.[56]

Given these sorts of claim from Blackwood and others, I believe that we can formulate divine self-sufficiency as follows:

> Divine self-sufficiency: A being is divinely self-sufficient if and only if that being's perfect essential nature is not dependent on, or derived from, anything external.

For the sake of clarity, it is worth emphasizing the difference between aseity and self-sufficiency. Aseity is a claim about the existence of God. Self-sufficiency is a claim about the *nature* of God. Given the classical theist's commitment to divine simplicity, aseity and self-sufficiency are identical to one another. However, other theists who reject divine simplicity do not need to make this identity claim. I believe that this identity claim is the reason why some contemporary proponents of classical theism believe that aseity and self-sufficiency entail impassibility, timelessness, immutability, and simplicity. In other words, they are smuggling in simplicity before laying out their arguments.[57]

§2.2 The Emotions of the Impassible God

What we have before us is the classical understanding of God. Now we must turn our attention to the classical doctrine of divine impassibility. Twentieth-century passibilist theologians frequently assert that the impassible God lacks any emotions, but this is a caricature. The classical tradition does affirm that God has emotions. Whatever emotions the classical God has, He has timelessly and changelessly. Classical theism affirms certain principles, assumptions, and divine attributes that other theists will deny. These other assumptions and attributes can explain why the impassible God cannot suffer.

To get us started in understanding these issues, I shall begin by focusing on the following definition of impassibility from James Arminius. He writes:

> IMPASSIBILITY is a pre-eminent mode of the Essence of God, according to which it is devoid of all suffering or feeling; not only because nothing can act against this Essence, for it is of infinite Being and devoid of external cause; but likewise because it cannot receive the act of any thing, for it is of simple Entity. Therefore, Christ has not suffered according to the Essence of his Deity.[58]

---

[56] (Blackwood 1658, 316).   [57] Cf. (Mullins 2018).
[58] (Arminius 1986, *Disputation* IV.XVII).

In order to gain some traction in our understanding of impassibility, it is worth summing up three common impassibility themes that make up the core of the doctrine. First, there is a widespread agreement that the impassible God cannot suffer. The "cannot" here is quite strong. It implies that it is metaphysically impossible for God to suffer.[59] Second, underlying this notion is the assumption that God cannot be moved, or acted on, by anything external to the divine nature. Again, the "cannot" is quite strong. It implies that it is metaphysically impossible for God to be moved, or acted on, by anything outside God.[60] Third, there is also a widespread agreement that God lacks passions, but this claim needs to be nuanced since there is disagreement among classical theists about the nature of passions. This disagreement makes it quite difficult to fully articulate the doctrine of impassibility.

What counts as a passion is a matter of dispute among the ancient and medieval theists.[61] The Western tradition shows an interesting variety of opinion on what counts as a passion. There are theologians who wish to say that mercy does not count as a passion, so God is merciful. Others, including Thomas Aquinas, hold that mercy is a passion and as such God cannot literally be said to be merciful.[62]

Another complication in fully articulating impassibility is with regards to the concept of emotion, which covers a wide range of affective states that include passions, but which is not reducible to passions. In reflecting on Latin theologians such as Augustine and Aquinas, Anastasia Scrutton suggests that we can place the classical understanding of emotions on a continuum. On one side of the continuum are passions that are involuntary, arational, and physical. On the other side of the continuum are what we today would call the cognitive emotions, which are voluntary, potentially rational, and nonphysical.[63] Classical theists are denying that God has passions in this sense, but they are not denying that God has the cognitive emotions.

This notion of a continuum helps gain some traction on understanding the classical doctrine of God, but there seems to be more at play. For example, the nineteenth-century theologian William Shedd denies that God has any passions, but he holds that God has two emotions: love and wrath. Shedd says that these two emotions are in fact one and the same moral attribute of God – holiness.[64] Shedd is not alone in affirming that God lacks passions, and yet is full of love and wrath. This is a fairly common claim throughout Church history, although not all agree that God literally has wrath.[65] The theme of divine wrath will be

---

[59] (Helm 1990, 120–1).   [60] (Creel 1997, 314).   [61] (Scrutton 2011, chapter 1).
[62] (Aquinas, *Summa Theologia*, 1.Q21.a3).   [63] (Scrutton 2011, 53).   [64] (Shedd 1888, 174).
[65] (Gavrilyuk 2004, 51–60).

discussed in Section 5. For now, I shall simply note that Shedd's claim fits with Scrutton's continuum.

How does a classical theist like Shedd go about deciding which emotions can truly be literally attributed to an impassible God? I focus on literal attribution because impassibilists have long held that various emotions predicated of God in scripture can be metaphorically attributed to God. It is worth noting that analogical and univocal predications of God are both literal attributions, not metaphorical.[66] The classical theist justifies the metaphorical attributions on the basis of what is literally true about God. What I am concerned with now is which emotions can be literally attributed to God – that is, emotions such as love and wrath. Answering this question will help one understand why the impassible God cannot suffer.

There are several inconsistency criteria that early and medieval theologians express that eventually become part of what later Christian theologians use to develop a clearer account of impassibility. Identifying these criteria will help us overcome the disagreement about passions and emotions among classical theists, and help us discern which emotional attributes can be literally predicated of an impassible God.

Some early Church fathers held that all passions are of a sinful nature or sinful disposition. Not all agreed. Some argued that only certain passions are of a sinful nature. All do agree, however, that God is morally perfect. Hence, one criterion is inconsistency with God's moral perfection.[67] Any passion such as lust, greed, or pride must be ruled out from being literally attributed to the morally perfect God. Call this the Moral Inconsistency Criterion.

> Moral Inconsistency Criterion: Any passion or emotion that is inconsistent with God's moral perfection cannot literally be attributed to God.

Another criterion relates to reason. Some fathers held that the passions are inherently irrational. According to this view, anyone who acts out of a passion must be doing so irrationally. The passionate person does not have her emotions lined up with reason. Such a person is out of control, and ruled by emotions instead of sober reason. However, other Church fathers held that not all passions are inherently irrational because emotions can motivate moral reasoning and action. All agree that God is perfectly rational. His actions are always in line with, indeed, identical to, His wisdom given divine simplicity. So another criterion is inconsistency with God's perfect rationality. Call this the Rational Inconsistency Criterion.

---

[66] (Muis 2011). [67] (Gavrilyuk 2004, 51).

Rational Inconsistency Criterion: Any passion or emotion that entails irrationality cannot literally be attributed to God.

Some theologians held that certain passions are morally and rationally neutral, while other passions are positive. For these theologians, God can have the positive passions, such as love, but cannot have the negative passions that imply sin or irrationality.[68] Even though there is a disagreement here over what counts as a passion, or even a negative emotion, a clear picture seems to emerge. God can be said to have whatever passions or emotions pass the Moral Inconsistency Criterion and the Rational Inconsistency Criterion.

This is a good start to understanding impassibility, but it is not the whole story since a passible God can satisfy these criteria. As we shall see, passibilists will say that God has an emotional responsiveness to creation, but never in a way that is immoral or irrational.[69] So more is at play in the classical tradition in trying to figure out which emotions can be literally attributed to an impassible God and which cannot. As I shall discuss later, the classical theist agrees with the passibilist about the cognitive nature of emotions. Emotions are cognitive in that they track the value of reality. Where the passibilist and impassibilist seem to disagree is over how God evaluates things. Understanding this emotional evaluation will help one understand why the impassible God cannot suffer.

§2.3 The Happiness of the Impassible God

There is a divine attribute that is often overlooked in contemporary discussions that will help us understand why the impassible God cannot suffer. It is an attribute that has wide affirmation in classical Christian theology. In the older theological texts, this divine attribute is often called God's *blessedness*. And it is also referred to as God's happiness, bliss, or felicity. According to Scrutton: "[T]he early church tended to see *apatheia* and/or blissfulness as an ideal on a 'metaphysical' as well as on a specifically moral level. Because passions were thought to be involuntary and to overcome reason, the experience of passions would disturb God's existence and bliss."[70]

What exactly is this attribute of divine blessedness? James Ussher explains it as follows: "It is the property of God, whereby he hath all fullnesse [sic] of delight and contentment in himself." According to Ussher, all felicity, happiness, endless bliss, and glory arise from God's perfect nature. So God has no need for anything else because He is perfectly happy in Himself. Ussher goes on to explain that, because God is perfectly happy, nothing outside God can move His will. With creatures like you and me, we are moved to act by external

---

[68] (Lister 2013, chapter 3) (Scrutton 2011, chapters 1 and 2).   [69] Cf. (Taliaferro 1989).
[70] (Scrutton 2011, 17).

factors. For example, if I see someone who is in a state of pure misery, I will hopefully be moved by this towards an action that will help alleviate this person's misery. Yet, according to Ussher, God is not like this. Since God is perfectly happy, He cannot be moved to act by anything outside Himself. Instead, God can only will to act towards His own glory.[71]

Before moving forward, it is worth pausing to reflect on several things. In particular, note the connection to the impassibilist claim that God cannot be moved by anything external to the divine nature. Ussher has not fully explained why this happy, impassible God cannot be moved by anything external to the divine nature. The passibilist might complain that such a God is failing to have emotional responses that properly track the values in reality. How can such a God know of the suffering of the world, and yet remain perfectly happy? The answer to this lies in the impassible God's timeless and immutable emotional evaluation of Himself.

Thomists have long reflected on divine blessedness, and it seems to me that one will find the answers we have been looking for here.[72] Like Ussher, Eric Silverman proclaims that God is the object of His own joy. How can this be? According to Thomists like Silverman, joy is an act of the will whereby one rests her will in a good object. On the Thomistic doctrine of God, God is identical to the supreme good. If God rests His will in Himself/goodness itself, then God will be infinitely happy. Because God correctly recognizes Himself to be the supreme and infinitely good object, He will rightly rest His will in Himself. Thus making Himself the object of His own eternal, immutable joy. Silverman explains that God cannot fail to be the object of His own joy because such a notion would be incoherent. If God somehow lacked infinite joy, Silverman says that this would indicate that God is deficient in His evaluation of Himself as the ultimate good. Surely an omniscient God would not be subject to such a deficient evaluation.[73]

To be clear, the impassibilist is claiming that God's emotional life does involve tracking the values in reality, and that God's emotions have an affect. Shedd is clear that happiness is a pleasurable emotion that arises from the harmony of the emotion with its proper object. In the case of the impassible God, Shedd says that the object of God's happiness is Himself.[74] The impassibilist is saying that, as the supreme good, God is the ultimate value in reality. God knows that He is the ultimate value, and has the proper emotional response to that value –that is, perfect happiness. Further, there is something that it is like for God to have this emotion – He has pure, undisturbed delight in Himself.

---

[71] (Ussher 1645, 34).   [72] (Aquinas, *Summa Contra Gentiles* I.90).
[73] (Silverman 2013, 168).   [74] (Shedd 1888, 174–7).

Yet this still does not fully explain why the impassible God cannot suffer. The passibilist affirms that God is the supreme good, the ultimate object of value in the world. Yet the passibilist affirms that God places values on creatures as well as His relationships with those creatures, which explains why God sometimes suffers. The passible God values His creation in that He sees His creatures as being worthy of His attention and action. What is the difference between the passibilist and the impassibilist here? The impassibilist believes that God's value swamps all of the value of created reality in a particular way. What that particular way is explains why God cannot be moved from His state of perfect bliss.

The claim from the impassibilist is that nothing external to God is of such value that God could possibly be moved to experience joy or sorrow because of it. If the impassible God were to be moved to experience sorrow for some created thing, the impassible God would be failing to properly evaluate that creature. The impassibilist is saying that God would be failing to properly evaluate that creature because God would be acting as if that creature has more value than the supreme good.[75] That is something that a proponent of impassibility will not allow for. As the omniscient supreme good, the impassible God cannot make such a deficient emotional evaluation. So the impassible God must be supremely blessed in Himself without any disruption to His perfect happiness.[76]

With this understanding of divine blessedness before us, one might ask how this helps us with articulating the doctrine of divine impassibility. Drawing on the Church tradition, Shedd offers the following criterion of blessedness to sort out which emotions can be attributed to God: "The criterion for determining which form of feeling is literally, and which is metaphorically attributable to God, is the divine *blessedness*. God cannot be the subject of any emotion that is intrinsically and necessarily an unhappy one."[77] Call this the Blessedness Criterion.

> Blessedness Criterion: Any passion or emotion that entails a disruption of God's happiness cannot literally be attributed to God.

In this Blessedness Criterion, one can find an explanation for why the impassible God cannot suffer. God cannot experience any emotion that conflicts with the proper emotional evaluation of Himself – that is, bliss. According to the impassibilist, it would be irrational and immoral for God to have the emotional evaluation of something external to God that would disturb His bliss. For

---

[75] (Wittmann 2016, 145).   [76] (Randles 1900, 43–5).
[77] (Shedd 1888, 174) Cf. (Gavrilyuk 2004, 51–62) for a discussion on divine anger and wrath.

example, Tertullian claims that God is perfect in all of His emotions such as mercy, gentleness, and anger. Yet, God experiences these emotions in such a way that it does not conflict with His perfect happiness.[78]

Conclusion

After locating impassibility within classical theism, I have tried to uncover the underlying reasons why the classical God cannot suffer. What this revealed are three criteria that the classical theist uses for determining which emotions can literally be predicated of God, and which emotions cannot be possessed by God. The impassibilist claims that God cannot have any emotions that are inconsistent with His perfect rationality, moral goodness, and blessedness.

3 The Passible God

In the previous section, I located impassibility within classical theism in order to uncover the classical criteria used to discern which emotions can literally be predicated of God. Uncovering these criteria led to the claim that the impassible God cannot suffer because the classical God is perfectly happy. In this section, I shall locate divine passibility within a position called *neoclassical theism*. I shall explain which of the three criteria the neoclassical theist can agree on for discerning which emotions can literally be predicated of God. Then I will consider the attribute of omnisubjectivity in order to explain why the passible God can suffer.

§3.1 Locating Passibility within Neoclassical Theism

One of the things that makes exploring divine passibility so difficult is that it can be located within divergent models of God. As I explained in the introduction, one can find Calvinists, Arminians, open theists, process theists, panentheists, and pantheists all affirming divine passibility. Proponents of divine passibility tend to reject the classical attributes of timelessness, immutability, and simplicity, but do not seem to be united on much else. For ease of exposition, I shall focus my attention on a model of God called neoclassical theism. Neoclassical theism is a model of God that rejects one or more of the classical attributes. This is because the neoclassical theist thinks that it is impossible for God to possess all the classical attributes.[79] However, she does not reject God's exhaustive foreknowledge of the future. The affirmation of exhaustive divine foreknowledge is what distinguishes neoclassical theism from open theism. Of course, this leaves open several options for how to understand divine

---

[78] (Mozley 1926, 38).   [79] (Timpe 2013, 202).

foreknowledge. A neoclassical theist can affirm Calvinism, Arminianism, Molinism, simple foreknowledge, or something else. The neoclassical theist also affirms that God and creation are ontologically distinct, and affirms the doctrine of creation *ex nihilo*, thus denying pantheism and panentheism.[80] Further, she rejects process metaphysics, and retains a more classical substance metaphysics, thus distinguishing neoclassical theism from process theology. With that being said, allow me to unpack a neoclassical understanding of the divine attributes.

Existence and Essence. Passibilists who are neoclassical theists typically agree with classical theists that God is a necessarily existent being whose existence and essential nature are not dependent on anything external to the divine nature. In other words, the neoclassical theist affirms that God is *a se* and self-sufficient. Where the neoclassical theist disagrees is over which attributes are included in God's essentially perfect nature. The neoclassical theist thinks that attributes such as timelessness, immutability, simplicity, or impassibility are not perfections. She does think that God's essential nature includes perfections such as omnipotence, omniscience, omnibenevolence, and freedom. As God is self-sufficient, she does not think that His essential properties and powers are derived from anything outside God.

The neoclassical theist also notes an important distinction between the possession of a power, and the exercise of a power. The claim from the neoclassical theist is that God possesses maximal power, but that God does not have to exercise that power in order to possess that power. God can freely exercise His power in many ways according to His wisdom and goodness.

Temporality. The neoclassical theist says that God is an eternal being in that God exists without beginning and without end. Necessary existence gives us an eternally existing God for free because necessary existence entails never beginning to exist and never ceasing to exist. Timelessness and temporality both agree that God exists without beginning and without end. However, timelessness adds that God exists without succession, whereas temporality affirms that God has succession in His life as He freely exercises His power. To exercise one's power is to actualize a potential to bring about some state of affairs that did not previously exist. When God freely performs an action, He does something new, and thus undergoes succession. So temporality has a nice fit with necessary existence, omnipotence, and freedom. The everlasting God undergoes various kinds of change over time as He expresses His essential nature in new ways in response to His creatures.

---

[80] Cf. (Mullins 2016b).

Mutability. With the rejection of timelessness comes the rejection of immutability. The neoclassical theist sees no need to affirm that God is immutable. Instead, she thinks that God's power and freedom entail the ability to change in certain respects, such as becoming the creator and savior of the universe. Often times, theologians worry that a mutable God could cease to be good, or loving, or somehow cease to exist. There is no good reason to think that any of this follows from mutability. Necessary existence prevents the mutable God from ceasing to exist. Further, God's self-sufficiency says that God's essential attributes are not dependent on or derived from anything outside of God. Essential properties and powers cannot be gained or lost precisely because they are essential and not accidental. What this means is that it is metaphysically impossible for the mutable God to cease to be maximally good, maximally powerful, and so on as He freely exercises these powers in various ways over time.

Unity. Neoclassical theists tend to find the doctrine of divine simplicity incomprehensible. The notion that all God's properties and actions are identical to one another is a bit much for some to swallow. Also, as I noted earlier, the neoclassical theist affirms that God's power and freedom entail the ability to actualize potential. This entails that God is not purely actual because God has the capacity to exercise or not exercise His powers as He sees fit. Neoclassical theists take this to be an advantage because they find the claim that God is purely actual to be inconsistent with God's freedom. Hence, neoclassical theists opt for divine unity instead. Although God's essential attributes are not identical, as unified they are coextensive and compossible.[81] As coextensive, one will not find God's power floating free from God's wisdom, neither will one find any of God's essential attributes floating free from God. As compossible, all of God's attributes are internally consistent with one another.

A further caveat is worth noting about divine unity. The doctrine of divine simplicity denies that God has any accidental properties, and entails that God is not really related to creation. Traditionally, classical theists would say that God does not have accidental properties such as *Creator* and *Lord*.[82] The neoclassical theist affirms that God is really related to His creation, and that God acquires accidental properties as He relates to His universe in new ways. When God freely creates the universe, God acquires the accidental property *Creator*. This is because acquiring the property *Creator* is the necessary consequence of God freely choosing to exercise His essential power to create a universe.

---

[81] (Mawson 2018, 53).   [82] (Augustine, *The Trinity* V.17.).

Passibility. Like the classical theist, the passibilist says that God's emotions are always rational and based on sound moral judgments.[83] She affirms both the Moral Inconsistency Criterion and the Rational Inconsistency Criterion. Where she disagrees with the classical theist is over the nature of divine blessedness and creaturely influence on the divine life.

Recall that impassibility says that it is impossible for God to be influenced by anything external to the divine nature, and that it is impossible for God to have any emotion that is inconsistent with undisturbed happiness. The passibilist disagrees. She maintains that God can be moved or influenced by things external to the divine nature. This is because God has willingly created a universe in which He is capable of responding to, and cooperating with, His creatures in order to satisfy His purposes for His creation. Given this, the neoclassical theist maintains that God is capable of suffering. The passibilist affirms that God is as happy as one can be in any given circumstance.[84] Yet, she claims that God's happiness is disturbed by what transpires in the universe because a morally perfect God cannot be unmoved by the evils of the world.[85] Thus, neoclassical theists reject the Blessedness Criterion because they think it is inconsistent with the demands of moral perfection.

When the passibilist affirms that God only has emotions that are moral and rational, she is also affirming that God can experience suffering. How is this so? Recall the discussion from Section 1 about emotions. Emotions are cognitive in that they are judgments about the world. Emotions can be rational or irrational depending on how well they track reality. Emotions allow one to perceive the value of objects in the world. An emotional response to an object is partly constituted by the way the individual perceives the value of the object. An object has value to an agent if she perceives it to be worthy of her attention, and worthy of her to act on behalf of the object. If an emotional response fails to properly track the value of the object, the emotional response is not rational. If an emotional response properly tracks the value of the object, the emotional response is rational.

The passibilist says that God cares deeply for the universe that He has made. He knows full well the value of the universe, and has declared it to be very good (Genesis 1:31). The passibilist further claims that God greatly values His covenant people. God considers His covenant people to be worthy of His attention and action, and as such God is emotionally responsive to them. When they are unfaithful to the covenant, God is grieved by their unfaithfulness because He correctly perceives the disvalue of their immoral actions. God's

---

[83] (Brasnett 1928, 16 and 21) (Peckham 2019, 99).   [84] (Brasnett 1928, 73).
[85] (Wolterstorff 2010, chapter 10).

grief is a rational and moral response to their behavior. Yet, when God's unfaithful people suffer, God feels sorrow for them because He cares for them, and wants them to flourish according to His covenantal promise.[86] The passibilist claims that God's emotional responses to these situations accurately tracks the values in reality, and so God's emotional experiences are rational and moral. In God's emotional responses to His creatures, He sometimes experiences suffering.

§3.2 Omniscience and Experiential Knowledge

The passibilist has more to say about the differences between her position and the impassibilist over the nature of God's knowledge. Recall that the impassibilist claims that God cannot be moved, or acted on, by anything external to the divine nature. This has a particular entailment for understanding God's knowledge. As I have discussed above, on classical theism, God's knowledge is in no way dependent on, or derived from, creation. Instead, the classical God has a perfect comprehension of His own nature, and thus God possesses all tenseless propositional knowledge. Passibilists have tended to find this account of omniscience less than satisfactory.[87]

The neoclassical theist will affirm that God has an exhaustive knowledge of all tenseless propositions, but she will also affirm that there is more to know in the world. As noted in the previous section, there is also knowledge to be had of tensed propositions. As God sustains the universe in existence from moment to moment, the truth values of tensed propositions will constantly be changing. God's knowledge of what was true, what is true, and what will be true, is constantly changing. Thus, God's knowledge will change over time. In knowing the truth values of tensed propositions, the neoclassical theist will say that her God knows more than the classical God. But the neoclassical theist will not stop here with God's knowledge. She says that there is more knowledge to be had than merely propositional knowledge.

An omniscient God is typically said to know the truth value of all propositions, but several philosophers and theologians have complained that this does not do justice to God's cognitive perfection.[88] There is more to know in the world than *de dicto* propositions. There is also knowledge by acquaintance, or experiential knowledge.

What is experiential knowledge? Propositional knowledge is knowledge that something is the case. Experiential knowledge is knowledge of "what it is like." There is a common story that philosophers tell about a scientist named

---

[86] (O'Connor 1998).   [87] (McConnell 1924, 290).   [88] (Nagasawa 2003).

Mary in order to explain the difference between these two kinds of knowledge. The story can go something like this.

> STORY: Mary has had a very unusual upbringing. She has been locked in a room her entire life, and this room is decorated in only black and white. Mary has never seen any other colors besides black and white. Mary has at her disposal reading material about the entire world outside her room. She has spent her life studying this material closely, and she knows a great deal about many different subjects. Yet Mary has a particular interest in roses. She reads everything that she can about roses. She comes to know all of the propositional facts about roses, yet she has never seen a rose in person. She knows that <roses are red>, but this concept of *red* puzzles her. So she reads everything she can about color theory in order to get a better grasp on redness. She eventually comes to know all of the propositional facts about the color red. Yet her curiosity still pulls at her. One day, Mary discovers a way out of her black and white room. A fellow scientist has heard of her bizarre living situation, and offers to break her out. She accepts the fellow scientist's offer, but on one condition – she wants to see a rose in person as soon as she is out. The fellow scientist smuggles Mary out of the room in a trunk under the cover of darkness. Once the fellow scientist feels that they are far enough away from Mary's captors, he opens the trunk and hands her a rose. For the first time in Mary's life she sees a rose in person. She sees the color red.

Ask yourself the following question: does Mary's knowledge grow when she sees the rose? There are a fair number of philosophers who would say yes. She has not grown in propositional knowledge, but she has grown in experiential knowledge. There is something that it is like to see the color red that Mary could not know by reading about color theory. There is something that it is like to see a rose, to smell its fragrance, to feel the weight of the rose in one's hand. This kind of experiential knowledge is not something that Mary had in her black and white room. The propositional facts do not capture all there is to know about the world. Thus, Mary has truly grown in knowledge.

The passibilist says that if there is this kind of experiential knowledge to be had in the world, then God must have it. An omniscient God must know all there is to know, and that includes knowing things other than mere propositions. God must have experiential knowledge as well. For example, when God creates the universe, there is something that it is like for God to experience creating a universe out of nothing. God's experiential knowledge grows as He freely exercises His power and brings about new states of affairs into existence. God comes to know what it is like to experience His creatures for the first time, and this experiential knowledge is not reducible to God's propositional knowledge.

§3.3 Divine Empathy

Just how much experiential knowledge God has is something that passibilists have yet to properly debate. For the purposes of this Element, I shall focus on one kind of experiential knowledge that passibilists have explored in some detail – empathy. Empathy is an interesting kind of experiential knowledge because it gives one an understanding of other people's conscious states. As Linda Zagzebski explains: "Empathy is a way of making the emotional states of others intelligible to us."[89] Zagzesbki thinks that empathy is an important kind of knowledge for one to have for several reasons. One such reason is that empathy allows one to make fair and accurate moral judgments of another person. Through empathy, one can gain a better understanding of another person. The empath comes to know how that person sees the world, and what she cares about. Moreover, understanding a person's emotions is the key to understanding what motivates her to act. This understanding of another person's emotions and motivations is why empathy plays an important role in making fair and accurate moral judgments about another person.[90]

In light of the importance of empathy, Zagzebski contends that God must have the attribute of *omnisubjectivity*. According to Zagzebski: "Omnisubjectivity is, roughly, the property of consciously grasping with perfect accuracy and completeness the first-person perspective of every conscious being."[91] Zagzebski claims that omnisubjectivity is entailed by God's omniscience or maximal cognitive perfection. Zagzebski holds that if God is going to be omniscient, then God must be able to consciously grasp the first-person perspective of every creature. In order to know the first-person perspective of every creature, Zagzebski says that God must have maximal empathy towards His creation.

What is empathy? A somewhat rough-and-ready account of empathy is that it is the transference of an emotion from one person to another. Yet this claim needs to be nuanced to distinguish empathy from emotional contagion.

Both empathy and emotional contagion involve a transfer of an emotion from one person to another. However, most philosophers agree that emotional contagion is not the same thing as empathy.[92] An emotional contagion can occur when a person unconsciously acquires an emotion like that of another individual. One example of emotional contagion is when one walks into a frenzied mob and just finds herself in a state of frenzy, anger, and agitation. Empathy, by way of contrast, is not an unconscious transfer of emotions.[93] Empathy involves an understanding of what another person is like, and being aware that your

---

[89] (Zagzebski 2008, 238–9).   [90] (Zagzebski 2016, 448).   [91] (Zagzebski 2008, 231).
[92] (Maibom 2017, 22).   [93] (Zagzebski 2008, 237–9).

emotions are not the same as the other person's emotions.[94] Yet, more needs to be said to properly understand empathy.

It can often be difficult to understand what empathy is because it has been described in so many different ways. Sometimes philosophers describe empathy as "the mechanism by which we imaginatively construct the feelings of others, and therefore are able to put ourselves in their shoes."[95] There are various ways to describe how this mechanism works through simulation, theorizing, and perception.[96] However, this does not seem to be empathy itself. Instead, this sounds more like a disposition to be empathetic. Recall from Section 1 that there is a distinction between dispositions and emotions. The same can be said for empathy.

Empathy is an epistemic state that one achieves. In particular, empathy is a kind of experiential knowledge of other persons. This epistemic state involves both cognitive and affective features. This epistemic state is distinct from the disposition, power, or capacity that one has to achieve a state of empathy. Empathy is achieved when one is consciously aware of how another person feels, and what it is like for them to feel that way.[97] To be more precise, I will use Sally and her son Ben again to help define empathy.

> EMPATHY: Sally empathizes with Ben if and only if (i) Sally is consciously aware that Ben is having an emotion, E, (ii) Sally is consciously aware of what it feels like to have E, and (iii) on the right basis, Sally is consciously aware of what it is like for Ben to have E.

Condition (i) is typically taken to be the cognitive component of empathy. One can be aware that another person is having an emotion such as anger, and yet fail to empathize with that person. Simply being aware that a person is having an emotion is not the same as understanding what it is like for them to have that emotion. For example, psychopaths can be relatively good at consciously grasping that other people are having particular emotions. Yet it is widely held that psychopaths are not great with the affective components of empathy, among other things.[98]

Condition (ii) is the affective component of empathy. It explains that Sally has an understanding of the phenomenology of certain emotions. She understands what it is like to have certain kinds of affect that go along with particular emotions. However, condition (ii) by itself does not give Sally empathy because she can have a grasp of the phenomenology of an emotion without empathizing

---

[94] (Ravenscroft 2017, 149).   [95] (Scrutton 2011, 77).
[96] Cf. (Spaulding 2017) (Gallagher 2017).   [97] (Zahavi 2017, 35).
[98] (Kauppinen 2017, 221) (Shoemaker 2017, 243–50). Cf. (Kennett 2017).

with anyone. For example, Sally can know what it is like to be sad without being aware of anyone else's being sad.

Condition (iii) is what ties the first two conditions together in order to achieve empathy. It explains that Sally understands what it is like for Ben to have his emotion. Notice that condition (iii) says that Sally comes to this understanding "on the right basis." By "right basis," I am referring to the justification Sally has for understanding Ben. I have left this intentionally vague because there are multiple theories of what would justify Sally's empathy. However, most accounts insist that Ben must play a causal or explanatory role in Sally's achieving a state of empathy with Ben. Something about Ben is what explains Sally's empathy. For example, one might think that the justification involves Sally perceiving that Ben is having an emotion such as sadness. Since Sally personally knows what it is like to be sad, she is able to make an inference to what it is like for Ben to be sad. Other accounts of justification might deny that Sally makes an inference, but instead say that she achieves empathy in a properly basic way through her concern-based construal of Ben.

Before moving forward, it is important to nuance this account of empathy in order to avoid common confusions that people often have about the nature of empathy. To start, it must be noted that an empath is consciously aware that she is trying on a copy of the other individual's perspective. Empathy is a way of acquiring an emotion like that of another person. The acquired emotion is not identical to the emotion of the other person, but it is similar enough to help the empath understand what the other person is experiencing.[99] Empathy does not entail that the empath's perspective becomes identical to the perspective of the other person.

There is one final caveat to add about empathy before moving on. In the case of humans, exercising one's capacity to empathize with another person can involve effort, and be cognitively taxing if one is not well practiced at being empathetic.[100] Also, in the case of humans, the accuracy of our empathy is often less than ideal.[101] However, in the case of an omnisubjective God, Zagzebski suggests that His empathy will have perfect accuracy, and it will not be cognitively taxing. Zagzebski says that God must possess something she calls *perfect total empathy*. This "is the state of representing all of another person's conscious states, including their beliefs, sensations, moods, desires, and choices, as well as their emotions."[102] Indeed, God will have perfect total empathy for all His creatures.

---

[99] (Zagzebski 2008, 238).   [100] (Spaulding 2017, 18).   [101] (Ta and Ickes 2017).
[102] (Zagzebski 2008, 241).

Where does this leave us with regard to the impassibility debate? Zagzebski notes that omnisubjectivity is incompatible with impassibility.[103] An impassible God is a being who is not moved by anything external, and an omnisubjective God is moved to some extent by creation. In order for God to have empathic knowledge of some other person, God's knowledge must be grounded in, and derived from that person. God's empathic knowledge involves God having an empathic perceptual experience of another person. The passibilist is not merely saying that God understands what it is like to be Sally in some abstract sense that does not involve any emotional engagement with Sally, if such a sense there be. Instead, the passibilist is claiming that God has a deep emotional engagement with Sally, and that there are certain things that God simply cannot know about Sally without actually empathically experiencing her. This is because empathic knowledge, like experiential knowledge in general, is a form of knowledge by acquaintance.[104] One cannot have such knowledge without being acquainted with the world in some way. Hence, God is moved by the world that He has created.

The passibilist has more to say about the way that God is moved by His creation. According to Zagzebski: "A person cannot empathize with an emotion or a sensation without feeling the emotion or sensation because a copy of an emotion is an emotion, and a copy of a sensation is a sensation."[105] Any copy of a creature's emotional suffering will be emotional suffering. As Zagzebski puts it: "[A] perfect copy of pain is surely ruled out by impassibility, as is a copy of every other sensation or emotion, whether positive or negative. A perfectly empathic being is affected by what is outside of him."[106] A perfect copy of a creature's emotional suffering would quite obviously disturb God's perfect bliss. It does not seem coherent to say that God is experiencing perfect, undisrupted happiness while also experiencing a perfect representation of emotional suffering, turmoil, and pain. Hence, an omnisubjective God cannot be an impassible God.

4 The Love of God

In the contemporary debate over impassibility and passibility, a great deal of reflection has focused on divine love. Anastasia Scrutton notes that twentieth-century passibilists have tended to argue that the nature of love entails the denial of impassibility.[107] A typical line of argument is that perfect love entails suffering with the beloved in certain circumstances.[108] For example, Thomas Jay Oord argues that the biblical definition of love is "to act intentionally, in

---

[103] (Zagzebski 2013, 45).   [104] (Zagzebski 2016, 442).   [105] (Zagzebski 2008, 242–3).
[106] (Zagzebski 2013, 44–5).   [107] (Scrutton 2013, 870).   [108] (Fiddes 1988, 16–25).

sympathetic/empathetic response to God and others, to promote overall well-being."[109] The passibilist argues that the current state of the sin-stained world contains many such circumstances where a perfectly loving God's response towards His beloved creatures must involve empathetic suffering.[110]

It is worth noting that this definition of love rules out impassibility from the start. This is because proponents of divine impassibility explicitly deny that God's love is responsive toward the values of creatures, and deny that God is literally empathetic or compassionate.[111] As such, impassibilists do not typically find this line of reasoning convincing because they wish to affirm a different conception of divine love that better supports their position. Yet, passibilists will balk at the suggestion that God can be loving in a way that is neither responsive to nor empathetic with creatures.

This would seem to put the debate between impassibility and passibility at a standstill. Scrutton explains that "arguing for either position from divine love has, so far, only resulted in a stalemate, since both arguments rest on opposing ideals of love." According to Scrutton, the passibilist will appeal to the lover who suffers with the beloved out of solidarity, while the impassibilist will favor the wise Stoic who is blissful and charitable in his actions.[112]

However, there might be a way to push this debate forward by seeing if the impassibilist and passibilist share some common ground over the nature of divine love. To this end, I shall examine the claim that the impassible God's love is unresponsive to the values of creation. This will help one see the stark contrast between impassibility and passibility over God's emotions. Then, I will offer a close examination of what the impassibilist calls *the two desires of love*. The classical theist thinks that God's love involves two different desires: the desire to promote the well-being of the beloved, and the desire for union with the beloved. These two desires can serve as a common ground between impassibilists and passibilists. With this common ground established, I shall argue that the impassible God cannot satisfy the desire for union with the beloved. Instead, I shall argue that only a passible God can satisfy the desire for union with the beloved.

§4.1 The Uninfluenced Love of God

Passibilists complain that the impassible God's love is unresponsive or uninfluenced by the values of creatures. Contemporary impassibilists will often claim that the doctrine of impassibility has been caricatured in modern debates.[113]

---

[109] (Oord 2010, 17) Cf. (Peckham 2015, chapter 5). [110] (Brasnett 1928, 118).

[111] (Bates 1999, 289) (Zanchius 1601, 357–8). [112] (Scrutton 2013, 872).

[113] For example, Richard A. Muller in the Foreword to (Dolezal 2017, ix).

They will deny the accusation that the impassible God is unloving, indifferent, and unresponsive.[114]

Far from being a caricature, the uninfluenced love of God is entailed by impassibility. One will recall that it is metaphysically impossible for the impassible God to be caused, moved, or influenced by anything external to the divine nature. This consequence is actually explicitly endorsed in some theological circles. In more Calvinist traditions, there is a significant emphasis on God's love being necessarily uninfluenced. In speaking about God's election, D.A. Carson says that: "The Lord did not choose Israel because they were choice; rather he set his affection on them because he loved them (Deut. 7:7–10). In other words, he loved them because he loved them: one cannot probe further back than that."[115] This claim might seem rather innocuous at first glance, but there is a subtlety here that should not be overlooked. Why, according to Carson, *did* God love Israel? God simply did love Israel. According to Carson, there is nothing about Israel that influences God's election of them. Israel, according to Carson, is not "choice." God simply declares that He will love Israel.

The passibilist will object at this point by saying two things. First, she can take issue with the biblical exegesis of the impassibilist.[116] She might say that the impassibilist is exaggerating the claims about God's love for Israel. This is because there are several biblical passages that show that God's valuing of Israel is rooted, in part, in Abraham's responsiveness to God's calling.[117] Second, the passibilist thinks that the impassibilist's claims make God's love utterly arbitrary, and downright irrational. This is because the passibilist believes that love necessarily involves believing that the object of one's love has value.[118] A passibilist can argue that if God does not love Israel because of Israel's value, then it would seem that God literally has no *reason* to love Israel. Most theists will find it hard to swallow the notion that God ever acts without a reason.[119] However, the impassibilist will insist that this understanding of God's love ensures that God is truly sovereign. Let us probe a bit more deeply into the impassible understanding of God's love.

Arthur W. Pink's classic, *The Attributes of God*, devotes a whole chapter to the nature of God's love. Like Carson, Pink focuses on Deuteronomy 7 for his reflections on God's love. Pink writes:

---

[114] (Silverman 2013, 166).

[115] (Carson 2000, 648). It should be noted that Carson rejects a classical understanding of impassibility. Nothing about his rejection matters for my argument in this matter. (Carson 2006, 165).

[116] (Peckham 2015, chapter 6).   [117] (Moberly 2013, 43–4).   [118] (Scrutton 2011, 135).

[119] (Rice 2016).

> The love of God is *uninfluenced*. By this we mean there was nothing whatever
> in the objects of His love to call it into exercise, nothing in the creature to
> attract or prompt it. The love which one creature has for another is because of
> something in the object; but the love of God is free, spontaneous, uncaused.
> The only reason why God loves any is found in His own sovereign will.[120]

Throughout Pink's chapter, he continually emphasizes that God's love is completely "uncaused" and "uninfluenced" by anything outside God. Pink says:
"God has loved His people from everlasting, and therefore nothing about the
creature can be the cause of what is found in God from eternity. He loves *from*
Himself: 'according to His own purpose' (II Tim. 1:9)."[121]

Pink's account has several important nuances that should be considered. For
example, Pink claims that God does not love us because we have loved Him
(1 John 4:19). This is fairly intuitive when connected with the fact that God's
love is eternal.[122] Since Pink affirms the doctrine of creation *ex nihilo*, he
affirms that there is a state of affairs where God exists without creation.[123] As
a classical theist, Pink says that this prior state of affairs is a timeless state of
affairs. Since neoclassical theists affirm creation *ex nihilo*, they will also believe
that there is a state of affairs where God exists without creation. A neoclassical
theist can say that this is a timeless or a temporal state of affairs, depending on
her beliefs about the philosophy of time.[124] Either way, the classical and
neoclassical theist agree that there is a state of affairs where God exists without
creation. Pink's point is this: prior to the act of divine creation, when God is
determining which world to actualize, there simply are no creatures around to
love God. So it cannot be the case that God loves a creature because that creature
first loved God. There simply are no creatures in existence to love God. The
neoclassical theist should be willing to concede this point to Pink to some
extent.

However, this claim is not strong enough for Pink. He goes further in saying
that God's love is completely uninfluenced. Pink writes:

> [A] precious truth. God's love for me and for each of "His own" was entirely
> unmoved by anything in us. What was there in me to attract the heart of God?
> Absolutely nothing. But, to the contrary, there was everything to repel Him,
> everything calculated to make Him loathe me – sinful, depraved, a mass of
> corruption, with "no good thing in me."[125]

---

[120] (Pink 1975, 77–8). [121] (Pink 1975, 78). [122] (Pink 1975, 78). [123] (Pink 1975, 9).
[124] Neoclassical theists are divided over whether or not God is temporal without creation, but are
united in affirming that God is temporal with creation. For example, William Lane Craig affirms
that God is timeless *sans* creation, but temporal with creation. I affirm that God is temporal prior
to, and without, creation. Cf. (Craig 2001) (Mullins 2014).
[125] (Pink 1975, 78). Cf. (Bates 1999, 289).

For Pink, God's love is "sovereign, under obligations to none, a law unto Himself, acting always according to His own imperial pleasure." God has no reason to love whom He chooses to love other than His own pleasure. "Because God is God, He does as He pleases; because God is love, He loves whom He pleases." Reflecting on Romans 9:13, Pink makes it clear that God has no reason to love Jacob more than Esau, and yet God does. "Why? Because it pleased Him to do so."[126]

At this point, I have a worry that I would like to express. The impassibilist places a huge premium on God's independence. For the impassibilist, it is not simply the case that God's existence and nature are not dependent on anything external. The claim is stronger in that nothing about God's existence, nature, emotional life, or will is dependent on anything external to God. Recall again the classical understanding of divine blessedness. God's happiness is dependent entirely on Himself. Nothing external can add to, or diminish, God's perfect happiness.[127] Yet, it might seem that Pink's statements here about Jacob and Esau conflicts with the divine blessedness. Something about loving Jacob *pleases* God. It sounds like God is deriving pleasure from Jacob. Surely, this sort of pleasure would be an influence on God.

Pink will deny that this pleasure influences God. According to Pink: "The sovereignty of God's love necessarily follows from the fact that it is uninfluenced by anything in the creature. Thus, to affirm that the cause of His love lies in God Himself is only another way of saying, He loves whom He pleases."[128]

How are we to interpret this claim from Pink? I think there are several things to be said about Pink's statement. First, to be sure, Pink is employing a biblical phrase. He translates Ephesians 1:4–5 as saying that God predestines according to the pleasure of God's will. So, on one level of analysis, when Pink uses the language of "divine pleasure" he is simply quoting scripture. However, on a deeper analysis, it seems to me that the mention of God's "pleasure" is not to be taken literally. If taken literally, it would entail that God is deriving pleasure from loving Jacob. That would run counter to the impassibilist claim about divine blessedness. It seems that the more charitable reading of Pink is to say that Pink is using "pleasure" in some sort of nonliteral way to indicate that God's love is completely sovereign, and utterly uninfluenced by anything *ad extra*. This is how other classical theists speak of God's pleasure when reflecting on passages such as Ephesians 1. What "God's pleasure" means is that God wills Himself, or God's consideration of Himself is the ultimate explanation of God's action. The classical theist says there is no other explanation for why God acts.

---

[126] (Pink 1975, 79).   [127] (Dolezal 2019, 21).   [128] (Pink 1975, 79)

A common claim among classical theists is that God wills Himself or His own goodness in all that He does.[129] This captures the classical claim that God can only have a will that is directed towards the greatest good, which is God Himself. As Augustus Strong explains, the goodness of creatures is insignificant when compared to the goodness of God. God can choose no greater end than Himself. In willing Himself, God is infinitely blessed. For Strong, this is why creation cannot add to God's happiness, and why the goodness of creation cannot factor in God's decision-making.[130]

In order to understand claims like these, it is worth keeping in mind the different attributes that the classical theist affirms, such as simplicity. A simple God's will is identical to God's essence and existence.[131] Since God's existence is absolutely necessary, God's will is absolutely necessary. Otherwise, God's will is not identical to God's existence. What this means is that God necessarily wills Himself. The object of His love cannot be anything other than Himself. This helps reinforce the classical claim that God's will is not influenced by anything outside Himself. It also brings up an important piece in the debate over God's love – God only loves Himself.

Following Augustine and many other classical theists, Herman Bavinck explains that God's love must only be "self-love." God's "absolute love of self is nothing but a willing of oneself."[132] Because God is absolutely perfect, Bavinck says that God:

> [C]annot and may not love anything else except with a view to himself. He cannot and may not be satisfied with anything less than absolute perfection. When he loves others, he loves himself in them: his own virtues, works, gifts. Hence, he is absolutely blessed in himself, the sum-total of all goodness, of all perfection.[133]

To be clear, classical theists like Bavinck are not saying that God loves creatures because of intrinsic values that creatures have in themselves. Indeed, he explicitly denies this.[134] For Bavinck, that would entail God's love being responsive to values that God does not possess, and that His blessedness is not fully satisfied in Himself. Instead, the classical claim is that God only loves the value of His perfect nature.

Passibilists commonly complain that the impassible God's self-love does not look like love at all.[135] The passibilist insists that God's love must be responsive to the values of creatures. Classical theists such as Bavinck reply that God's self-love implies love for creatures.[136] It is a bit difficult to make sense of this

---

[129] (Dodds 2008, 173) [130] (Strong 1907b, 397–9). [131] (Charnock 1864, 387).
[132] (Bavinck 1979, 227). [133] (Bavinck 1979, 204). [134] (Bavinck 1979, 228).
[135] (Oord 2010, 67–8). [136] (Bavinck 1979, 228).

notion given the uninfluenced love of the impassible God. However, the idea seems to be something like this: God loves creatures in the sense that creatures are able to participate in God's perfect nature. Even though the impassible God is not responding to anything in or about the creature, the classical theist insists that creatures are able to benefit from God's perfect nature when they instantiate properties like goodness, power, and knowledge. To be sure, passibilists are not typically satisfied with this reply, but space limitations do not permit a further exploration of this issue.

I wish to consider one final issue from Pink's treatment of God's love that is relevant for seeing the differences between passibility and impassibility. Pink asks us to consider a possible world in which God's love is influenced. In this thought experiment, Pink considers the possibility that God's love is influenced by considerations that are external to the divine nature. Here is Pink's objection in full:

> For a moment, assume the opposite. Suppose God's love were regulated by anything else than His will: in such a case He would love by rule, and loving by rule He would be under a law of love, and then so far from being free, God would Himself be *ruled by law*. "In love having predestined us unto the adoption of children by Jesus Christ to Himself, according to" – what? Some excellency which He foresaw in them? No! What then? "According to the good pleasure of His will" (Eph. 1:4, 5).[137]

It is worth noting how deeply uninfluenced God's love is on Pink's account. God's love is completely, and utterly uninfluenced by anything *ad extra* to God. Not even some foreseen excellency in creatures can influence God's love. This is truly an uninfluenced, and uninfluenceable, God.

This is quite different from what the neoclassical theist has to say. The neoclassical theist says that God does consider the values of possible universes prior to His act of creation. The values of these possible universes influences God's decision as to which universe to select for creating. The neoclassical theist does not see this as some external law that rules God. Rather, she sees the consideration of values as part of the analysis of what it means for God to be loving and wise in His act of creation. For example, she will say that because God is perfectly good, God cannot create universes that are overwhelmed by evil. It is God's own essential goodness that delimits the range of possible universes that God can create. It is not some external law that floats free from God that is telling God what to do. Thus, she sees no loss in God's sovereignty in affirming that God considers the values of possible creatures when He selects which kind of universe to create.[138]

---

[137] (Pink 1975, 79).   [138] Cf. (Kraay 2010).

§4.2 What Is Love? The Search for Common Ground

What we have before us are two competing visions of God's love. The classical theist says that God's love is completely unresponsive to the value of creatures. The neoclassical theist says that God's love is responsive to the value of creatures. Which understanding of divine love is to be preferred? It might seem that we have come to a stalemate between the two positions because each will favor her own understanding of divine love. What is needed is some sort of common ground between the two positions that will help push the discussion forward.

Thankfully, some common ground can be found. Eric Silverman, and other classical theists, explain that love involves two desires. First, a desire to will the good for the beloved, and, second, a desire to will union with the beloved.[139] For the sake of argument, I think that the passibilist can grant the impassibilist that love involves these two desires. With this common ground on the nature of love, I believe that the debate between passibility and impassibility can move forward. As I shall argue, the passibilist seems to have an easier time satisfying the desire for union with the beloved because she affirms that God has empathy, whereas the classical theist denies that God has any empathy towards His creatures. Call this the Unity Problem for divine impassibility. I shall articulate the Unity Problem later. First, however, I must explore the two desires of love.

§4.2.1 The Desires of Love

In her recent work, *Wandering in Darkness*, the classical theist Eleonore Stump develops one of the most nuanced and detailed accounts of the desires of love in the contemporary literature.[140] Thus, I will focus my attention on her analysis of the two desires.

The first desire of love is a desire for the good of the beloved. Goodness is being used here broadly to cover different kinds of goods related to morality, beauty, and metaphysics.[141] The good of the beloved is objective in that there is something objectively good for a person based on her nature. The "good of the beloved has to be understood as that which truly is in the interest of the beloved and which truly does conduce to the beloved's flourishing."[142]

With regards to humans, a person can flourish in a variety of ways. She can flourish by growing in wisdom, moral knowledge, and virtue. A human person can also flourish by growing in physical strength and health, or by learning a new skill. So when it comes to promoting the good of a human person, one has

---

[139] (Silverman 2013, 171). Cf. (Aquinas, *ST* II, II.27.2) (Randles 1900, 53).
[140] (Stump 2010, 91).   [141] (Stump 2010, 93).   [142] (Stump 2010, 93).

a variety of potential actions to perform that would be conducive to the flourishing of the beloved. For example, a set of parents might wish to see their daughter grow in wisdom, so they hire her a personal tutor to help her with her homework. Or perhaps the parents have a child with a stunted emotional development, so they take their child to see a specialist who can help their child grow in emotional knowledge and sensitivity.

There is more nuance to Stump's account than I am offering here related to the epistemic limitations of human persons, and distinctions between intrinsic and derivative goods. Also, on Stump's account of love, anything that contributes to the objective good of the beloved draws the beloved closer to God.[143] Although interesting, a full discussion of such things would take us off track for the purposes of this Element. So I shall move on to consider the second desire of love – union with the beloved.

Union of love requires two things: personal presence and mutual closeness.[144] Personal presence is a necessary condition for mutual closeness, so I shall discuss it first. Personal presence comes in degrees. In order to be minimally present a person must be aware of another individual, and see him as a person. This other individual must be conscious and functioning relatively well.[145] This is not a particularly interesting kind of presence for Stump's purposes. Sally could be aware that Ben is in the room with her, but not have any particular concern or affection for Ben. Further, Ben could be completely unaware of Sally. In this situation, Sally is minimally present to Ben.

In order to develop this account of union, Stump says that we need *significant* personal presence. For significant personal presence, Stump says we must add something called *joint* or *shared attention*. Let us return to Sally. Say that Sally is aware that Ben is in the room, and does have some degree of concern towards Ben. Further, say that Ben is aware of Sally, and gestures emphatically towards a toy that he wants Sally to pick up. As Sally turns her attention towards the toy, she and Ben are both aware of one another, and yet they are both focused on the toy. They are aware that the other is focused on the toy. This kind of awareness is known as shared attention. As Stump points out, shared attention comes in degrees.[146] What ultimately matters for our purposes here is that shared attention involves a mutual awareness between two or more people that each of them is aware of the other as a person, and that each exhibits some degree of concern towards the other.

Recall that union requires personal presence and mutual closeness. With a discussion of personal presence on the table, we can turn our attention towards

---

[143] (Stump 2010, 93).   [144] (Stump 2010, 109).   [145] (Stump 2010, 112).
[146] (Stump 2010, 113–18).

mutual closeness. As already noted, shared attention comes in degrees. The richer the shared attention is between two persons, the greater their mutual closeness will be.[147] Yet Stump says that more is needed. One necessary feature of mutual closeness is an openness of mind. This is where one person is open and willing to share her important thoughts and feelings with another person. Not any old thought will do, however. Most people who know me are aware of my love for delectable cheeseburgers. I have even discussed my love for these delectable cheeseburgers in several of my writings. So one does not have to be particularly close to me to know this fact about my life. Knowing this fact about me does not really shed much light on who I am as a person. But there are other facts about me that I am not willing to share with just anyone. These are facts that I share only with a select few. If I were to share these facts with you, I would be actively revealing my innermost thoughts, desires, and passions with you. This sort of active self-revelation is one of the necessary components of mutual closeness that Stump has in mind.[148]

Again, more is needed for *mutual* closeness. Say that I am on a date, and I believe that it is going quite well. I decide to share some of my innermost thoughts, thoughts that are really important to me. If my date shows no interest in this self-revelation, there will not be another date. Why? Because the potential for mutual closeness seems dim. In order for the closeness to be mutual, my date will need to show an interest in my self-revelation. She has to exhibit an ability to comprehend, and a willingness to receive what I am sharing with her.[149] These claims about comprehension and willingness need to be unpacked a bit further.

Consider first comprehension. If my date is unable to comprehend what I am revealing to her about myself, the potential for closeness in our relationship will be quite minimal. Comprehension comes in degrees, and comprehension involves more than mere propositional knowledge. My date could have a great deal of propositional knowledge about me, but that does not mean that she really knows me. Perhaps she stalked me online before agreeing to go on a date with me. During her internet search she could acquire a fair bit of propositional knowledge about me, but she will not know me in the deepest sense. She will not know what it is like to experience my presence, witness my quirks and mannerisms, or hear my laugh. She will also not have a deep understanding of my mental states, and the emotional weight or subjective value that I place on certain things in my life. In order to know me in the deepest way, she needs to be able to get into my shoes, and see things from my perspective. In other words, she needs to have some degree of empathy and emotional intelligence in order to

---

[147] (Stump 2010, 119).   [148] (Stump 2010, 120).   [149] (Stump 2010, 120).

understand my perspective on the world. She does not have to agree with my perspective on various things, but she must have some comprehension of what it is like to be me in order to be close to me. I, in turn, must have the same comprehension of her in order for the closeness to be mutual.

This capacity to understand another person in this deep way is one thing, but there needs to be a willingness to open one's self to this kind of closeness. Say that my date has a highly refined capacity for empathy, and a staggering emotional intelligence. She is able to comprehend my self-revelation to her. Yet, say that she is unwilling to accept my self-revelation. Perhaps I misjudged the situation, and she is really not that into me. In revealing myself to her, she might have no interest in being that close to me. Without her willingness to accept what I am revealing about myself, there can be no mutual closeness between us.

This willingness component of mutual closeness can be quite scary. There is a kind of vulnerability that comes with this openness of mind. As Stump explains, a person makes herself vulnerable to her beloved in the very act of opening up. In revealing my innermost thoughts to someone, I am demonstrating my desire for union with this person. The satisfaction of that desire is now in her hands.[150] I might make myself an open book to my date, and she might show a willingness to understand who I am as a person, but then reject what she sees in me. This rejection can come in several different forms, and each comes with varying degrees of associated pain. For instance, a person might be put off by my love of heavy metal. So, once this person willingly comes to know who I am, she might decide that she is no longer willing to be close to me, and the satisfaction of my desire to be close to her is now cut off.

This discussion of mutual closeness brings up issues related to experiential knowledge of other persons as discussed already. In the next section, I shall try to bring these threads together and develop the Unity Problem for divine impassibility. Before doing so, however, I wish to note some worries that a classical theist will face.

Given the discussion in Section 4.1, one might be unwilling to grant that the classical God can satisfy the desires of love because the classical God cannot have any desires for anything other than Himself.[151] In fact, classical theists tend to deny that God even has desires because God is perfectly satisfied in Himself,[152] thus making the whole discussion of desires of love a nonstarter for the classical theist. Further, it is difficult to see how a timeless and immutable God could satisfy a desire of love because desire satisfaction quite clearly entails change from *having a desire* to *satisfying a desire*. In order to avoid

---

[150] (Stump 2010, 122).   [151] (Hasker 2016, 723).   [152] (Lindberg 2008, 7–8).

this problem, a classical theist might try to say that God analogically has desires. However, the idea of timelessly and immutably having a desire that is also timelessly and immutably satisfied does not sound like an analogical use of desire. Instead, it sounds incoherent, which is why most classical theists tend to deny that God has desires. However, I shall set those worries aside, and focus on the Unity Problem.

§4.3 The Unity Problem

Stump makes it clear that unity and mutual closeness can be hindered by the makeup of one or more parties in the loving relationship.[153] For instance, there might be something wrong with Sally that prevents her from drawing closer to God. Perhaps some horrible sin she refuses to repent of, or perhaps some lack of trust in God grounded in previous experiences of betrayal by loved ones. But what about the other way around? What if there is something wrong with God that prevents Him from being united to us?

The classical theist will wish to say that there is nothing wrong with the impassible God, but the passibilist will beg to differ. Allow me to explain. According to Stump, the intrinsic characteristics of the lovers will determine the character and extent of union that is possible.[154] One might complain that the impassible God is going to be severely limited in the possible extent of His union with creatures compared to the possible extent of union between a passible, omnisubjective God and His creatures.

Recall that a lover cannot be fully, or perfectly, unified with her beloved if she does not have the deepest possible epistemic understanding of her beloved. As Zagzebski makes clear: "Love is premised on understanding the other, and the fuller the understanding, the greater the possibility for love."[155] As noted earlier, unity comes in degrees. Also, epistemic comprehension or understanding comes in degrees.[156] Surely an omniscient God has complete epistemic understanding. Surely in the eschaton God will be fully unified with His beloved creatures. So God will have a complete epistemic understanding of His creatures.

In order to have a complete epistemic understanding, God will have to understand creaturely mental states. Recall that one of the conditions for unity with the beloved is the ability to comprehend the beloved's mental states, and the emotional weight or subjective value that the beloved places on certain things. If God is going to have the kind of comprehension needed for unity, God will need to have empathy. One cannot have this kind of comprehension without

---

[153] Cf. (Stump 2018).   [154] (Stump 2010, 99).   [155] (Zagzebski 2016, 449).
[156] (Roberts and Wood 2007, 43).

empathy. As should be clear by now, an omnisubjective God can have this kind of comprehension. According to Zagzebski, the "omnisubjective God is the most intimately loving because he is the most intimately knowing."[157]

An impassible God, by the same token, cannot have empathy in any meaningful sense of the term. Classical theists, like Anselm, explicitly deny empathy and compassion of the impassible God.[158] As the impassibilist Girolamo Zanchius makes clear, empathy can bring suffering, and this is something an impassible God cannot do. This is because an impassible God is perfectly happy, and nothing can disturb God's perfect happiness.[159] So it would seem that impassibility prevents God from being able to comprehend His creatures, and thus prevents God from being united with His creatures in love.

Consider the following example to see how an impassible God is prevented from being fully united with His creatures in love. An impassible God can know all of the propositions about His creatures. For instance, an impassible God will know that Sally has mental states x, y, and z. He will also know that Sally places a certain amount of emotional weight or subjective value on these mental states. Say that Sally has certain mental states associated with her son Ben. Perhaps mental states such as "I love my son Ben," and "I would do anything for Ben." Ben is currently suffering from cancer, and is on death's door. Naturally, Sally is in emotional anguish. She is deeply disturbed by what is happening to her son because she has placed a great amount of emotional weight or subjective value on her son.

An impassible God can know all of the propositional facts about Sally and her current mental and emotional state. However, can an impassible God be united in love with Sally? The answer is "no" since an impassible God cannot satisfy the conditions of comprehension needed for mutual closeness. Mere propositional knowledge is not enough for comprehension. Knowledge of what it is like to be Sally is also needed for comprehension, and an impassible God cannot have that kind of knowledge. As I shall argue, an impassible God fails to satisfy the conditions of comprehension in at least two ways.

§4.3.1 The Impassible God Cannot Comprehend Suffering

The first reason that the impassible God cannot satisfy the conditions for mutual closeness is because the impassible God cannot comprehend what it is like to suffer, and thus cannot comprehend what it is like to be Sally in her suffering. An impassible God cannot suffer because an impassible God is necessarily in a state of undisturbed bliss. For such a God, it is metaphysically impossible for Him to comprehend what it is like to be Sally in her situation of agony. Sally is

---

[157] (Zagzebski 2016, 450).   [158] (Anselm, *Proslogion* VIII).   [159] (Zanchius 1601, 357–8).

in a state of deep mental anguish, and that is a mental state that an impassible God cannot possibly understand.

Recall that the classical theist maintains that God has a perfect cognitive grasp of His own nature. In grasping His own nature, God experiences perfect, undisturbed bliss. Thus, the impassible God knows that it is metaphysically impossible for Him to suffer.[160] As Randles explains: "Perfect blessedness excludes everything contrary to happiness." Any "happiness mingled with unhappiness is imperfect blessedness."[161] For Randles, the impassible God cannot have any hint of uneasiness, conflict, weakness, limitation, or sorrow in His emotional life since such a thing is incompatible with perfect blessedness.[162] Any experiential knowledge of "suffering would be a loss of inherent excellence, and is therefore impossible to Him who is absolutely perfect."[163]

Thus, the impassible God is a God who cannot comprehend what it is like to be Sally in her suffering. Comprehension of Sally's emotional states is necessary for mutual closeness. So the emotional life of the impassible God prevents Him from possessing mutual closeness with Sally.

§4.3.2 The Impassible God Cannot Be Moved

There is a second reason that the impassible God cannot comprehend what it is like to be Sally, and thus is prevented from enjoying mutual closeness with her. Recall from Section 2.3 that it is metaphysically impossible for an impassible God to be moved or acted on by anything outside God. His emotional state of perfect happiness is based entirely on Himself. Since an impassible God's emotional state is based purely and entirely on Himself, it is metaphysically impossible for an impassible God to comprehend what it is like to have one's emotional states wrapped up in another person. As Randles explains: "The happiness of God is from the perfection of His nature independently of all other beings ... it is not in the power of the creature to spoil or diminish His infinite blessedness."[164] To further drive home the impassible God's emotional independence from creatures, Stephen Charnock reminds us that it is impossible for creatures to add to, or subtract from, the infinite blessedness of God as well.[165]

An impassible God cannot possibly comprehend what it is like for Sally to place the emotional weight or subjective value that she does on her son Ben because it is metaphysically impossible for God to have His emotional states

---

[160] (Silverman 2013, 168).   [161] (Randles 1900, 43–4).   [162] (Randles 1900, 48).
[163] (Randles 1900, 50).   [164] (Randles 1900, 44).
[165] Stephen Charnock in (Renihan 2015, 144–54). Cf. (Ussher 1645, 35).

depend on something external to the divine nature. It is metaphysically impossible for an impassible God to be emotionally invested in another person because such an investment would render God's emotional life dependent on something *ad extra* to the divine nature. Such a dependence would be in clear violation of divine impassibility. So an impassible God cannot possibly understand what it is like to be Sally in her emotional vulnerability towards her son.

§4.3.3 Responding to Possible Rejoinders

The Unity Problem arises from an internal conflict between impassibility and the desire for union with the beloved. An impassibilist might try to respond to the Unity Problem by saying that an impassible God can understand what it is like to be Sally without God's ever having to experience suffering. I find this suggestion implausible. The impassible God is necessarily in a state of undisrupted, and undisturbable, joy. The suggestion that such a being could possibly understand what it is like to experience suffering seems like it deserves nothing more than an incredulous stare. This is so because such a being has never once suffered, neither can such a being ever suffer. How could such a being possibly understand what it is like to be Sally in her suffering?

However, the impassibilist might try to argue that some person P could have an understanding of what it is like to suffer without ever having suffered. Perhaps something like the following story will get your intuitions pumping in the impassibilist's favor:

> STORY: Imagine that the universe popped into existence only five minutes ago. The universe came into existence with all the appearance of age, including a whole host of memories and psychological states, etc., that lead the inhabitants of the universe to believe that it is in fact 13.5 billion years old. Imagine that Bill finds himself in this universe with the distinct memory of having his foot caught in a bear trap fifteen years ago. The memory of this experience does not cause Bill any pain or discomfort at present. However, Bill does understand what it is like to experience having his foot caught in a bear trap.[166]

The impassibilist might insist that Bill understands what it is like to suffer even though his understanding of suffering is not based on any actual experience of suffering. The goal of this thought experiment is to give the impassible God comprehension of Sally's suffering without God's actually experiencing Sally or her conscious states in order to help the impassible God satisfy the desire for union with the beloved. The passibilist finds this suggestion to be

---

[166] Thanks to Peter van Inwagen for this colorful thought experiment.

perplexing to say the least. This is because there is a deep disanalogy in the thought experiment between Bill and God.

In the thought experiment, Bill is not in an analogous epistemic situation to that of an impassible God. Even though Bill does not actually experience suffering, Bill is at least capable of suffering. The ability of Bill to suffer is one way a philosopher might try to justify the claim that Bill understands what it is like to suffer.[167] Thus, one point of disanalogy is this: Bill has the ability to suffer whereas the impassible God lacks the ability to suffer. Yet there is another point of disanalogy: an omniscient and impassible God knows that it is metaphysically impossible for Him to suffer. The impassible God can never be in the same epistemic state as Bill because He knows His nature well enough to know that such a thing is impossible. What this means is that the Unity Problem remains.

§4.4 Love Rhymes with Sympathy

Given the failures of impassibility to satisfy the conditions for mutual closeness, the possible unity between God and Sally seems quite limited, if not impossible. Things are quite different for a possible God who enjoys omnisubjectivity. A possible God can enjoy a range of emotions that are consistent with God's rational and moral nature. A possible God with the capacity for maximal empathy can understand what it is like to be Sally, and so can enjoy a deep epistemic comprehension of her. Thus making the possible God able to enjoy a significantly deeper degree of unity with Sally than an impassible God. Zagzebski goes so far as to say "that omnisubjectivity is a condition for the perfect love God has for us."[168]

Francis McConnell agrees that the empathy of God is needed in order to have a fully loving God. He claims that a God who cannot suffer with and for His creatures is morally lower than the thousands of men and women who have willingly suffered for the well-being of others. He writes: "There is no way for God to escape sorrow if he is a God of love. We must repeat that we are not trying to glorify suffering on its own account, but we are trying to preserve the moral fullness of the Divine Life."[169]

According to McConnell, the passibilist is not claiming that there is some intrinsic virtue in God suffering simply for the sake of suffering. Instead, the Christ-like God sympathetically suffers in order to reconcile creatures to Himself. As McConnell explains: "If we are to reconcile men to the God of pain, we must show that God does not ask men to undergo experiences which he

---

[167] Cf. (Nagasawa 2008, 64–71). [168] (Zagzebski 2016, 449).
[169] (McConnell 1924, 287–8).

is not, as far as possible, willing to undergo himself."[170] This is because humans "want to feel that their suffering means something at the center of the universe. It means that they crave at least to be understood through the understanding which comes out of sympathetic sharing of distress."[171] God and humanity bear the cross with one another. "It is cross-bearing together which provides the closest unions between man and God." For McConnell, this union may start in pain, but it ends in an abiding joy in the eschaton.[172]

5 The Wrath of God and Other Moral Judgments

In most theistic religions, it is believed that God is the ultimate moral judge of the universe. One common theological claim is that there will come a day when God will judge the righteous and the wicked. God's wrath will be poured out on the wicked, and divine justice will reign. Divine wrath is also closely related to other theological themes such as God's patience and mercy, His promises to help those in need, and His promises to offer salvation to humanity. These theological claims about God's wrath, mercy, and promises of salvation are wrapped up in the notion that God is a morally perfect judge. God judges that it is just to pour out His wrath on certain individuals, and God judges that it is good to offer mercy and promise salvation to humanity. Since emotions are evaluative judgments, emotions play a significant role in one's moral reasoning. In fact, some philosophers will claim that there can be no moral reasoning without emotions.

The relationship between emotions and moral reasoning has several potential implications for understanding God's moral judgments. In this section, I shall examine a few possible implications for God's judgments related to His wrath, mercy and compassion, and promise of salvation. I will discuss possible problems for both the impassible and passible views of God. First, however, I must lay out the scriptural basis for understanding God's wrath, patience, and compassion.

§5.1 Divine Wrath, Patience, and Compassion

Given that my main area of expertise is Christian theology, I shall focus primarily on the Hebrew Bible and Christian New Testament. The concept of divine wrath is a major theme in the Hebrew Bible that is described over 400 times.[173] This theme is picked up in the New Testament as well. This scriptural basis serves as a common ground between impassibilists and passibilists for the Christian doctrine of God. Both sides of the debate wish to properly capture

---

[170] (McConnell 1924, 289).   [171] (McConnell 1924, 290).
[172] (Lane 2001) (McConnell 1924, 293).   [173] (Lane 2001, 149).

the biblical description of God's wrath. What is not yet clear is which side can best capture the biblical teaching. Before delving into that debate, it will be helpful to get a better understanding of how each side describes God's wrath.

According to Tony Lane, the biblical concept of God's wrath is as follows:

> It is God's personal, vigorous opposition both to evil and to evil people. This is a steady, unrelenting antagonism that arises from God's very nature, his holiness. It is God's revulsion to evil and all that opposes him, his displeasure at it and the venting of that displeasure. It is his passionate resistance to every will that is set against him.[174]

As one might expect, Lane thinks that God's wrath is incompatible with impassibility because this involves God being displeased, and thus not experiencing perfect, undisturbed happiness.[175] Of course, the classical theist Arthur W. Pink agrees with Lane that divine wrath is a major biblical theme that must be included in one's doctrine of God. Pink even uses similar language to describe God's wrath. Pink says:

> The wrath of God is His eternal detestation of all unrighteousness. It is the displeasure and indignation of Divine equity against evil. It is the holiness of God stirred into activity against sin. It is the moving cause of that just sentence which He passes upon evildoers. God is angry against sin because it is a rebelling against His authority, a wrong done to His inviolable sovereignty. Insurrectionists against God's government shall be made to know that God is the Lord.[176]

Again, one can see that both sides of the debate wish to affirm the wrath of God. Yet it is not clear how both sides can properly make this affirmation. How can Lane and Pink have similar descriptions of God's wrath, and yet differ over impassibility? One might think that a classical theist like Pink is speaking metaphorically about God's wrath, whereas a passibilist like Lane is speaking literally about God's wrath. However, as we saw in Section 2, classical theists such as William Shedd affirm that God literally has the emotion of wrath. Pink agrees and says that God cannot be morally perfect if He does not have the attribute of wrath.[177] Thus, it might seem like a metaphorical wrath is not an option for impassibility. I shall take up the issue of literal and metaphorical wrath later on in this section. For now, I shall work with the assumption that the classical theist and neoclassical theist both wish to capture the biblical portrayal of God's wrath as literally as possible.

What is the biblical portrayal of God's wrath that both sides wish to affirm? It is worth noting that God's wrath is often connected to God's patience and

---

[174] (Lane 2001, 154).   [175] (Lane 2001, 148).   [176] (Pink 1975, 83).   [177] (Pink 1975, 83).

compassion in scripture (for example, Exodus 34:6–7). In the Bible, God's wrath or anger is not an irrational, knee-jerk reaction. Instead, God's anger is often portrayed as rational and patient because God's anger is never separated from His love.[178] This is dramatically portrayed in Hosea 11 where God's compassion towards Israel is the reason God changes from a plan of wrath to a plan of mercy. Reflecting on the Old Testament theme of divine repentance, or change, R.W.L. Moberly explains that the meaning of such passages is clear: "YHWH's sovereignty is not exercised arbitrarily, but responsibly and responsively, interacting with the moral, or immoral, actions of human beings."[179] Moberly takes God's moral responsiveness to be an axiom within the Hebrew understanding of God.[180] The takeaway from this is that, biblically, God's compassionate responsiveness towards creatures plays a significant role in His moral judgments. Biblically, God will not pour out His wrath without first engaging in compassionate reasoning. As John C. Peckham explains: "[T]he biblical language of *compassion* explicitly depicts 'suffering along with,' akin to sympathy/empathy, that is, [a] responsive feeling of emotion along with and for the object of compassion."[181]

This raises an obvious problem for the classical theist. Such compassionate responsiveness is not open to the impassible God who cannot be moved or influenced by anything external to the divine nature. As Anselm makes clear, an impassible God cannot have compassion.[182] As Pink reminds us: "It is not the wretchedness of the creatures which causes Him to show mercy, for God is not influenced by things outside of Himself as we are."[183] It would seem that there is a conflict between classical theism and the biblical portrayal of God's anger and compassion. In the next section, I shall make this conflict more apparent.

§5.2 The Problem of Divine Wrath

As already discussed, the classical theist denies that God literally has the emotion of compassion. However, as mentioned earlier, classical theists such as Shedd affirm that God literally has the emotion of wrath. According to Pink, God cannot be morally perfect if He does not have the attribute of wrath.[184] In Pink's mind, if one is not willing to reflect on "God's detestation of sin," then one does not have a heart with the proper attitude towards all of God's perfect attributes.[185]

This being the case, I wish to focus on a problem for classical theism from divine wrath. As we have seen, the classical theist believes that the impassible

---

[178] (Peckham 2015, 126–7).   [179] (Moberly 1998, 114).   [180] (Moberly 2013, 108–37).
[181] (Peckham 2015, 178).   [182] (Anselm, *Proslogion* VIII).   [183] (Pink 1975, 74).
[184] (Pink 1975, 83).   [185] (Pink 1975, 84–5).

God cannot be influenced by anything external.[186] If the impassible God is truly such that He cannot be influenced by anything external, it seems quite difficult to understand how such a God could have wrath. God's wrath, just like His love, should be uninfluenced and nonresponsive to creatures. Otherwise, the impassible God will be dependent on creatures for how He feels. This problem for classical theism can be articulated as follows:

1) God has the emotion of wrath.
2) If God's wrath is caused or influenced by creatures, then God's wrath is dependent on creatures.
3) God's wrath is caused or influenced by creatures.
4) Thus, God's wrath is dependent on creatures.

As stated before, (1) is a major biblical theme, and most classical theists are committed to the claim that God is literally wrathful; (2) is a premise that impassibilists and passibilists agree on; (3) seems fairly obvious, otherwise, who is God's wrath directed towards?, and (4) is an entailment from (1)–(3), and clearly violates impassibility's claim that God cannot be dependent on anything *ad extra* for His nature, knowledge, will, and feeling. The classical theist must do something to avoid (4). If the classical theist wishes to avoid (4), she will need to reject one of the previous premises. But which one? In what follows, I will explore some possible options for the classical theist, and argue that these options will be to no avail.

§5.2.1 Deny that God Has Wrath

One option for the classical theist is to deny (1) because it lacks nuance. The classical theist can say that God does not literally have the emotion of wrath.[187] Instead, she can say that God metaphorically has wrath. This move, however, faces two difficulties. First, the overwhelming biblical data on God's wrath does not seem to be merely metaphorical. Second, the task of describing what is God's wrath a metaphor for.

I'll start with the biblical data. The Bible clearly portrays God as being angry, and experiencing the negative affect of wrath.[188] Psalms 7:11 says: "God is a righteous judge, and a God who feels indignation every day." It seems fairly obvious that the feeling of indignation is incompatible with the perfect blessedness of classical theism. Thus, the classical theist will have to say that this indignation is merely an anthropopathic description of God. She will have to say that passages such as Psalms 7 do not literally describe God's emotional life, but

---

[186] (Creel 1986, 11).   [187] (Randles 1900, 41–2).   [188] (Peckham 2015, 125).

instead somehow really teach God's impassible wrath. What that impassible wrath looks like will be discussed in the next subsection.

To be clear, the classical theist will have to explain away every instance of divine wrath in scripture as anthropopathic. The passibilist will complain that this is quite a lot of scripture to explain away. The classical theist has to explain away over 400 passages that would be much more naturally interpreted along passibilist lines. Given that divine suffering is another major theme in scripture, a passibilist will say that there simply is no biblical justification for interpreting all of the wrath passages as anthropopathic.[189]

The passibilist can concede that if there were some biblical support for the doctrine of divine impassibility, then one might have some justification for interpreting all of these passages as anthropopathic. The problem is that impassibility does not seem to have any biblical support. For example, consider the New Testament scholar Michael F. Bird's *Evangelical Theology*. Throughout the majority of Bird's textbook, he offers a careful discussion of scripture as it pertains to each topic. Yet, when it comes to impassibility, he offers nothing. Bird considers several other divine attributes and offers at least some biblical references for each. Impassibility is the only attribute that he considers where he does not give any biblical reference in support.[190] Why? According to passibilists like John Peckham, it is because there is no biblical support for impassibility.[191]

The next difficulty that this strategy faces is developing an account of divine wrath as a metaphor. What could these divine wrath passages be a metaphor for? Some classical theists say that these biblical passages are a metaphor about God's underlying moral principles for judging sinners and saints without any perturbation in God's bliss. Unrepentant sinners experience God's love *as if* it were wrath, but wrath is not actually an attribute of God.[192] This gives us a metaphorical strategy to consider.

Marshall Randles adopts a metaphorical strategy like this. Randles says that the biblical phrases about divine wrath must be taken in a way that does not carry any meaning that would conflict with God's perfect happiness.[193] He says that God's wrath may be understood as God's pleasure at the prevalence of right against wrong. Randles says: "[T]here is a sense in which He must have satisfaction in His condemnation of sin, and overthrow of its power."[194] For Randles, what is denoted by "God's wrath" is really God's judicial attitude that condemns sin and punishes sinners. Although scripture speaks of God being displeased or feeling indignation, Randles maintains that we cannot take this to

---

[189] Cf. (Fretheim 1984).   [190] (Bird 2013, 130–1).   [191] (Peckham 2019, 43 and 92).
[192] Cf. (Mozley 1926, 105–9) (Gavrilyuk 2004, 55–8).   [193] (Randles 1900, 42).
[194] (Randles 1900, 40).

mean that God's perfect happiness is in anyway disturbed. Instead, he claims that we should take these biblical phrases about God's being agitated to indicate the moral principles by which God is actuated towards offenders. He also describes God's wrath as the disposition of a moral ruler to condemn or punish.[195]

At first glance, this might seem to be consistent with impassibility because Randles has maintained God's undisturbed happiness. However, Randles has said that the biblical claims about God's emotional life should be understood as "the moral principles by which He is actuated towards offenders, rather than passionate feeling. But whatever of feeling may be intended, it can imply nothing contrary to infinite happiness."[196] Consider this statement carefully. God is *actuated* towards offenders. This is not obviously consistent with divine impassibility. To be actuated is to be motivated by something. In this instance, it would seem that Randles is saying that God is motivated by sinners to perform certain actions. Yet, divine impassibility says that God cannot be subject to any influence from anything *ad extra* to the divine nature. As the classical theist, James E. Dolezal, reminds us: "Our sins, be they ever so many, have no effect on God."[197] Thus, Randles' statement is not consistent with divine impassibility. He has not escaped the argument because he is still affirming (3) in a sense that allows the argument to move forward. His interpretation of the biblical passages still leads to a God who is causally influenced by His creatures to act in a certain way – that is, to metaphorically have the emotion of wrath. Thus, Randles' interpretation has not escaped my argument against impassibility.

§5.2.2 Deny that God's Wrath Is Caused by Creatures

Another option is for the classical theist to reject (3) in the argument. Shedd, like any classical defender of divine impassibility, claims that God is not passively affected by the universe. The things that transpire in the universe cannot cause God to suffer and be moved. God is always self-moved because God is self-sufficient. However, contrary to Shedd, it seems like the sin of human persons is influencing God. Consider again God's happiness. Given divine simplicity, God is happiness. The object of God's happiness is Himself. As such, God's happiness is not dependent, effected, or brought about by something outside of God. When it comes to God's wrath, however, the object clearly seems to be something outside of God for God cannot be the proper object of wrath. Shedd, like many theologians, claims that God does have wrath that is directed towards the unrighteous.

---

[195] (Randles 1900, 40–1).   [196] (Randles 1900, 41–2).   [197] (Dolezal 2019, 23).

Surely this wrath demonstrates that God is affected by the world such that God would unleash His wrath on the unrepentant. It is the sins of humanity that invokes God's wrath. Recall Pink's statement from before: "God is angry against sin because it is a rebelling against His authority, a wrong done to His inviolable sovereignty."[198] That directly conflicts with the notion that God is impassible. So the classical theist must say something else. She must say something similar to the claims she made with regards to God's uninfluenced love. In other words, nothing that I am, and nothing that I do causes God to be angry. God's wrath is completely uninfluenced by my sin, lest He be dependent on me.[199]

To avoid this dependence, the classical theologian must say that the creature is not the cause of God's wrath. How can she say that? One possible move is to say that God's wrath is dependent on His eternal knowledge of what creatures will in fact do. Consider the proposition <Sally kicks a puppy at time t_x>. Perhaps the classical theist can say that God knows this proposition eternally, and this proposition is the basis of His wrath directed towards Sally. The proposition, and not the creature, is the basis of God's wrath. The classical theist will need to say more in order to avoid making God's wrath dependent on anything *ad extra* to the divine nature. For instance, the classical theist will need to maintain that propositions do not exist independently of God. Perhaps she will say that all propositions exist in the mind of God. This is a popular move in church history, and is sometimes called the doctrine of divine ideas. Most classical theists will already be committed to this move.

The classical theist will need to do more, however, than simply place propositions into the mind of God. The classical theist must give an account of the truthmakers for these propositions. Allow me to explain. Many contemporary discussions on the freedom–foreknowledge problem maintain that God can know the future, and that humans can have free will despite God knowing their future free actions. Various solutions to this problem involve maintaining that human persons are the truthmakers for these eternal propositions. God knows that Sally will kick a puppy before Sally does, in fact, do so. However, nothing about God knowing this causes Sally to kick the puppy. This is because Sally is the truthmaker for the proposition about her kicking the puppy.

If a classical theist holds to this solution to the freedom–foreknowledge problem, she will not be able to escape my argument against impassibility. If Sally is the truthmaker for the proposition <Sally kicks a puppy at time t_x>, then Sally will be responsible for that proposition's being true. Since this proposition is an idea in the mind of God that means that Sally is responsible for God's

---

[198] (Pink 1975, 83).　　[199] (Arminius 1986, Disputation IV.LIII).

having the beliefs that God in fact has. Thus, God's knowledge will be dependent on Sally. That goes against divine impassibility since impassibility explicitly says that God's knowledge is not dependent on anything *ad extra*. Further, in making Sally the truthmaker, one will have made Sally responsible for God's wrath. God's wrath is grounded in His knowledge, and His knowledge is grounded in Sally. Hence, God's wrath is grounded in Sally. Therefore, God's wrath is dependent on something *ad extra* to the divine nature.

How might the classical theist avoid this? It seems that the classical theist could deny that Sally is the truthmaker for these eternal propositions in the mind of God. She will have to say that God is the truthmaker for these propositions in order to avoid saying that something *ad extra* to the divine nature influences God's wrath. But that would seem to lead to theological determinism – the view that God determines everything that happens in the world.[200] Theological determinism is difficult to square with human free will and moral responsibility, although some Calvinists might not be bothered by this.

For those Calvinists who are not bothered by divine determinism, I would like to raise a problem for adopting this related to divine impassibility. In making these moves, one will have successfully ensured that God's wrath is not dependent on anything *ad extra* to the divine nature. However, that means that God's wrath is dependent on Himself. God is the proper object of God's wrath! That seems counterintuitive. God is perfectly good, so it cannot be the case that God is the proper object of God's wrath.

I am not certain what the proponent of divine impassibility can say at this point. It seems implausible to say that God is the object of God's wrath. Yet the impassibilist cannot say that creatures cause or influence God's wrath. That also seems implausible. The claim that the sins of humanity in no way influence God's wrath is not one that I expect most theologians are willing to endorse. However, that seems to be the only option for the classical theist. Again, recall the statement from the contemporary classical theist, James Dolezal: "Our sins, be they ever so many, have no effect on God."[201]

§5.2.3 The Passibilist Solution

Since the neoclassical theist denies impassibility, she has no problem in affirming (4). The neoclassical theist says that God's wrath is dependent on sinful creatures. God would not have wrath without their existing proper objects of God's wrath. God's emotional life over time is partly dependent on creatures, but His existence is in no way dependent on creatures. The passible God existed in a state of bliss before creating the universe. The passible God's emotional life

---

[200] (Pereboom 2016).   [201] (Dolezal 2019, 23).

changes as He interacts with His creation, but His necessary existence is in no way threatened by this.

The divine passibilist Francis McConnell explains that God's moral nature is unchanging, and thus God's moral nature demands that God change His actions towards humans as humans change their own actions over time.[202] A perfectly good God will treat sinful human persons differently than He treats repentant human persons. God has an attitude of moral disapproval towards human sin, but He will rejoice when sinners repent (Luke 15).

The passibilist can agree with the classical theist that God has an unchanging will to treat sinners and saints according to the dictates of morality. The passibilist agrees that God's will with regard to morality does not change. Since neoclassical theism can be affirmed by Calvinists and Molinists, there are several ways to develop this idea. She can affirm a doctrine of God's eternal and unchanging decrees for creation if she wants. This can be based on God's middle knowledge if she affirms a Molinist doctrine of God's omniscience. If she is a Calvinist, she will not base this on middle knowledge.

Where the neoclassical theist parts ways with the classical theist is over God's changing affections and actions as He deals with creatures. Say that God eternally decrees to forgive all those who seek repentance. This decree will remain unchanging as God interacts with His creatures over time. What the neoclassical theist affirms is that God cannot pour out His forgiveness on creatures until the right moment in time when creatures ask for forgiveness. The neoclassical theist has no problem affirming this because she thinks that God is temporal, mutable, and passible. She thinks that God can change in regards to His affections and actions towards creatures from one moment to the next.

§5.3 Can the Passible God Be Trustworthy in His Moral Judgments?

Not every philosophical theologian will be happy with this passibilist solution. Classical theists have long complained that the passible God cannot be a morally trustworthy God.[203] In the remainder of this section, and in the next, I shall consider some of these kinds of objections to divine passibility.

The classical theist Stephen Charnock thinks that a passible and mutable God cannot be a proper moral judge. According to Charnock, a passible and mutable God changes in His knowledge, and so must be an unfit object of our trust. This is because a being who changes in knowledge cannot be trusted to make sound promises and moral judgments.[204] He claims that: "A changeable mind and

---

[202] (McConnell 1927, 81).   [203] (Dolezal 2017, 19).   [204] (Charnock 1864, 385).

understanding cannot make a due and right judgment of things to be done and things to be avoided. No wise man would judge it reasonable to trust a weak and flitting person."[205]

It seems to me that Charnock has two underdeveloped arguments here. I will do my best to develop his arguments, and offer a response in favor of possibility.

§5.3.1 Untrustworthy Promises

It seems that the first argument that Charnock is trying to develop is that a possible and mutable God cannot make trustworthy promises. Charnock says that a being who changes in knowledge may make promises that are reasonable now, but those promises might later turn out to be unfit to perform.[206] Charnock does not give us any examples, but the idea seems to be intuitive. Surely many of us have found ourselves in the situation that Charnock is describing. The idea seems to be this:

> UNTRUSTWORTHY: A God whose knowledge changes over time might make a mistake. Say that God makes a promise at a particular time based on what He knows to be true at that time. At that point in time, it is a perfectly reasonable and good promise to make. However, as history unfolds, unforeseen things happen that now make the promise impractical or immoral to keep. This is a common experience in our creaturely lives, and surely we will wish to say that God is not subject to this sort of problem. Surely we will wish to say that God's promises are trustworthy, and will not become impractical or immoral for God to keep in the future.

Is the passible God subject to untrustworthy promises? I cannot see how He is. The neoclassical theist can adopt a Molinist or a Calvinist approach to divine foreknowledge and providence. On Molinism and Calvinism, God will know the tenseless truths about the universe that He is actualizing. God grows in His knowledge of tensed facts as history unfolds, but His knowledge of all the tenseless facts stays the same. God will also grow in His experiential knowledge as history unfolds, but again, His knowledge of the tenseless facts does not change. The neoclassical theist can say that God's promises are based on what He knows the future will hold, so there is no worry that God will make a promise that will later turn out to be impractical or immoral to keep. So whichever way a passibilist wishes to go with regards to God's foreknowledge and providence, it seems that the passible God is perfectly capable to make trustworthy promises.

---

[205] (Charnock 1864, 385). Cf. (Randles 1900, 25).

[206] (Charnock 1864, 385). Cf. (Mawson 2008).

§5.3.2 The Incompetent Judge Problem

Charnock says that a God who changes in knowledge is an incompetent judge. Such a God could threaten a punishment that seems appropriate at the time, but then later discover that the threatened punishment is unjust.[207] Like Charnock's previous argument, he does not give us any details, but I find the idea somewhat easy to grasp. Many of us have had the experience that Charnock is pointing toward. There are many examples in everyday life where a punishment seems appropriate at the time, but later on we come to see that the punishment is deeply unfair.

However, I don't see why one should think that divine passibility is subject to this problem. As McConnell explains, many of the objections to a mutable and passible deity are based on the inability to think of changefulness apart from fleeting whim. True, human persons do tend to change their mind on a whim, but McConnell thinks we have no reason to believe that a morally perfect God is like that.[208] According to Richard Swinburne, a perfectly good God has the knowledge and power to perform the best action in any given circumstance. Assuming, of course, that there is a best action in any given circumstance. It might not always be the case that there is a best action in particular circumstances. In those cases, God always does morally great actions that further the completion of His ultimate purpose for creation.[209]

Again, on neoclassical theism God, has an exhaustive knowledge of how the future will in fact unfold according to His decree of a particular universe. The neoclassical God has more than enough knowledge to make sound moral judgments. Nothing about God's growing in knowledge with regards to experience and tensed facts would render God unable to make sound moral judgments. With knowledge like that, there is nothing in the world that could change in such a way that would render God's prior moral judgments unjust.

6 Divine Empathy and the Problem of Creepy Emotions

Sometimes contemporary passibilists who are process theists will say that God shares all the feelings of all others even more fully than we do.[210] Think about that for a second. God shares every emotion we have. Without any nuance, this claim could lead to some pretty obvious objections. Richard Creel comically points out one such objection: does that mean that God feels horny?[211] Now, I doubt that Creel will say that there is something wrong with feeling horny per se. It really depends on the context. Yet, there seems to be something creepy about an omnipresent, omniscient, horny God. Especially given that the process

---

[207] (Charnock 1864, 385).   [208] (McConnell 1927, 73).   [209] (Swinburne 2016, 146–9).
[210] (Hartshorne 1964, 14 and 259).   [211] (Creel 1986, 129).

theist takes the world to be God's body. To be sure, the neoclassical theist does not affirm that the universe is God's body as the process theist does. Yet one might still think that something has gone wrong here with possibility because it seems to give us a God with all sorts of creepy emotions. In this section, I shall explore this problem in more detail, and discuss two ways for passibilists to respond.

§6.1 What Is the Problem for Divine Empathy?

One might try to develop objections to divine possibility by saying that the Moral Inconsistency Criterion or the Rational Inconsistency Criterion rules out God's having empathy. Consider a classic version of this objection from Creel. He says that God cannot take joy in all that creatures enjoy, or sorrow in all that creatures sorrow in. Creel explains that such a view is too simple because such a God "must rejoice with the sadist while the sadist tortures his victim, and grieve with the sadist when his victim dies and can no longer be tormented. But surely God is no more obligated than we are to share in the joys and sorrows of a demented mind."[212] Creel says that God cannot be subject to such a mistaken emotional evaluative judgment so as to take joy in what the sadist takes joy in.[213] That would render God immoral and irrational.

I believe that Creel thinks the passibilist is presupposing a simplistic view of divine empathy. The simplistic view of divine empathy can be stated as follows:

> Simplistic Divine Empathy: (i) God feels exactly what His creatures feel, and (ii) God agrees with the emotional evaluation of His creatures.

Condition (ii) is the force behind the sadist example. Creel is saying that God cannot have the same emotional judgment as the sadist. According to Creel, if God did share in the joy of the sadist, God would not be just.[214]

However, it is possible to interpret Creel's "sharing" as something else based on other examples he uses against possibility, such as feeling stupid or feeling horny.[215] With these examples, Creel can be understood as saying that God cannot share a creature's emotion in the sense of merely feeling exactly what she is feeling. These examples don't have to involve God agreeing with the creature's emotional evaluation of the situation. Instead, the claim seems to be that God understands the emotion without agreeing with the judgment of the emotion, and that there is something unseemly about God's understanding this emotion.

I suggest that there are at least two possible arguments here that a classical theist might develop against divine possibility based on the moral and rational

---

[212] (Creel 1986, 118).   [213] (Creel 1986, 118).   [214] (Creel 1986, 132).
[215] (Creel 1986, 129).

inconsistency criteria. Each argument attacks a different condition of the Simplistic Divine Empathy thesis. Call the first argument, the *Problem of Emotional Agreement.*

> The Problem of Emotional Agreement: Some creatures that God would empathize with are sadists. A God who is morally perfect cannot have the same emotional evaluation as the sadist. Thus, the passibilist should reject condition (ii) of Simplistic Divine Empathy.

Call the second argument, the *Problem of Mere Feeling.*

> The Problem of Mere Feeling: Some creatures that God would empathize with feel horny and stupid. Perhaps there is nothing immoral about God feeling horny per se, but it certainly appears to be creepy for God to be horny. So creepy that it verges on the immoral. Whatever one thinks of horniness, it is certainly irrational for God to feel stupid. Thus, the passibilist should reject condition (i) of Simplistic Divine Empathy.

These two arguments appear to cause serious trouble for the passibilist because there is no empathy left if the passibilist rejects conditions (i) and (ii). How is the passibilist going to avoid the Problem of Emotional Agreement and the Problem of Mere Feeling? In what follows, I shall offer two options for the passibilist to avoid God having creepy emotions.

§6.2 The Zagzebski Option

If the neoclassical theist affirms that God is omnisubjective, she will be affirming that God has perfect total empathy with all of His creatures. God has a complete and accurate representation of all of His creatures' conscious states, including the emotions of the sadist and the lustful wanton. Linda Zagzebski is aware of these sorts of objections, but finds them unpersuasive because she rejects the Simplistic Divine Empathy thesis that the problems are built on.[216]

Zagzebski can say that condition (i) is too ambiguous to capture the nuance of real empathy. As discussed in Section 3, empathy involves a person consciously acquiring a copy of another person's emotion, and being aware that your emotions are not the same as the other person's emotions.[217] Thus, contrary to condition (ii), the empath never gives up her own perspective when empathizing with another person. When you try on someone else's emotional shoes, your own shoes are not far behind. Also, as noted in there, Zagzebski takes empathy to be a prerequisite to sound moral judgments. Without perfect empathy, God cannot properly agree or disagree with a human person's emotional perspective

---

[216] (Zagzebski 2016, 447).   [217] (Zagzebski 2016, 442) (Ravenscroft 2017, 149).

on the world.[218] Far from entailing agreement, empathy presupposes that disagreement is possible.

Return to the example of the sadist in the Problem of Emotional Agreement. A passibilist like Zagzebski could say something like the following:

> REPLY: God will possess a perfect copy of the sadist's conscious states. God will understand what it is like for the sadist to delight in torturing the innocent. As perfectly rational, God will know that He is not the sadist. Thus, in empathizing, God is not violating the Rational Inconsistency Criterion. Further, in empathizing, God will not agree with the sadist that delight is the appropriate emotion to have. Empathy is achieved by God coming to understand what it is like for the sadist to feel as she does, but God's emotional life does not stop at merely empathizing with the sadist. Instead, God will have an emotional response that is consistent with His moral perfection. This will most likely be wrath towards the sadist. Without having this perfect empathy with the sadist, God would not be able to accurately judge the sadist. Instead of empathy being inconsistent with God's moral perfection, God's moral perfection demands that God have perfect empathy. Thus, the omnisubjective God can satisfy the Moral Inconsistency Criterion, the Rational Inconsistency Criterion, and avoid the Problem of Emotional Agreement.

That is how a passibilist such as Zagzebski can respond to the Problem of Emotional Agreement.

What about the Problem of Mere Feeling? Zagzebski admits that her position will not satisfy someone who thinks that there are intrinsically immoral emotions, and that consciously representing them is itself intrinsically immoral. As she comments: "On this view God would be contaminated by his own creatures if he really grasped what it is like to have their bad feelings."[219] As Zagzebski understands the objection, if God has too close of a contact with His creatures by empathizing with them, God would no longer be perfect. Zagzebski states that she finds this sort of objection implausible, and out of step with Christian theological doctrines like grace, providence, and sanctification. She says little by way of explicating this, but she thinks that God's love is premised on God having a complete empathetic understanding of His creatures. Thus, she suggests that: "Sanctification may involve a breaking down of the barriers between human life and divine life so that, when a human being shares in the divine life, God also shares in our own lives."[220]

Given the introductory nature of this Element, perhaps it is best to leave Zagzebski's suggestion as a possible way for the passibilist to develop a response to the Problem of Mere Feeling. In the next section, I shall

---

[218] (Zagzebski 2016, 448).   [219] (Zagzebski 2016, 449).   [220] (Zagzebski 2016, 449).

consider a different way for the passibilist to respond to the Problem of Mere Feeling.

§6.3 The Maximal God Option

Most passibilists will accept something like a Zagzebski-style response to the Problem of Emotional Agreement because they reject the mistaken notion of empathy that the problem is based on. However, even with a proper understanding of empathy in place, a passibilist might still have worries about the Problem of Mere Feeling. Perhaps one is not convinced by Zagzebski's way out because one still thinks there is something creepy about an omnipresent being understanding what it is like to be horny, or understanding what it is like to be filled with hatred towards one's enemies. To be fair, the omnisubjective God does not agree with every emotional perspective of His creatures, but He does have a perfect grasp of the affects and sensations of these emotions. God knows what it is like for His creatures to be horny, and knows what it is like for His creatures to hate their enemies.[221] If a passibilist is put off by this suggestion, she can say that there is something incoherent with omnisubjectivity because it violates the Moral Inconsistency Criterion. Instead, the passibilist can adopt a weaker thesis about God's maximal knowledge. In order to understand this, I need to introduce a few concepts.

Zagzebski is working from the framework of perfect being theology. In several places, she argues that omnisubjectivity is a property that it is better to have than not have. The "better to have than not have" is a standard premise in perfect being arguments. However, there is an ambiguity in perfect being theology. There are two different ways of understanding God's perfection.

Perfect being theology starts by defining God as the greatest metaphysically possible being.[222] In order for God to be the greatest metaphysically possible being, God must possess all of the possible great-making properties, and enjoy these great-making properties to the greatest consistently possible degree of intensity.[223] Most of the discussion within perfect being theology takes place over determining which properties are the great-making properties, and whether or not those great-making properties are coherent. Great-making properties are properties that it is better to have than not have. They are properties that make its possessor intrinsically great, and not merely great relative to some circumstance.

Yujin Nagasawa points out that perfect being theologians often assume something called the Omni-God thesis.[224] On the Omni-God thesis, God's

---

[221] (Zagzebski 2013, 46–8).   [222] (Nagasawa 2017, 9).   [223] (Nagasawa 2017, 64).
[224] (Nagasawa 2017, 25).

perfections are properties like omnipotence, omniscience, and omnibenevolence. In this case, the intensity of the great-making properties is interpreted as meaning all powerful, all knowing, and all good. Nagasawa points out that perfect being theology need not be committed to the Omni-God thesis. Instead, one can affirm the Maximal God thesis, which says that God has the maximally consistent set of power, knowledge, and goodness.[225] The Maximal God thesis is, in principal, consistent with the Omni-God thesis because it may turn out that the maximally consistent set of power, knowledge, and goodness is omnipotence, omniscience, and omnibenevolence. However, the Maximal God thesis is a weaker claim than the Omni-God thesis because it might turn out that an attribute like omnipotence is not metaphysically possible since it contains some incoherence within the concept.

Here is the payoff for the neoclassical theist. A neoclassical theist might say that the concept of omnisubjectivity is incoherent because it is inconsistent with God's moral perfection. She might say that God cannot have a perfect grasp of *all* conscious states of creatures because the possession of certain conscious states is immoral, irrational, or perhaps just creepy. Yet, she can maintain the claim that God has maximal empathy, even if she denies that God is omnisubjective. In this case, the passibilist would be saying that God has empathy to a degree of intensity that is maximally consistent with God's moral and rational perfection. There seem to be several ways to develop this line of thought.

Earlier I noted that some passibilists believe that God feels everything that creatures feel, yet He feels these emotions even more fully than we do.[226] This sort of passibilist view seems to be saying that God has a perfect cognitive grasp of all creaturely emotions, and that God grasps the affect of the creaturely emotions to a greater intensity than any creature. A neoclassical theist who adopts a maximal God approach can reject this claim. She can say that God has a deep cognitive grasp of all creaturely conscious states, yet God does not have the affect of the emotions of His creatures to the full range of intensity. On this view, God has a perfect understanding of His creatures' evaluative judgments, but His grasp of the affects of their evaluations can only extend so far. God understands what it is like for His creatures to hate their enemies, yet the intensity of the affect of this hatred is not something that God can fully grasp. Perhaps this is because God's love prevents Him from fully feeling the intensity of hatred. In this way, one can say that God has the maximal degree of empathy and knowledge that is consistent with God's perfect moral character.

This seems to be the way that the passibilist Bertrand R. Brasnett understands God's knowledge. According to Brasnett: "We may posit emotion and passion

---

[225] (Nagasawa 2017, 92).   [226] (Oord 2019a, 52).

at the very centre of the divine being, provided always that the emotion is good and the passion righteous." For Brasnett, there is a wide range of conscious states that God can empathize with. However, there are pleasures creatures take joy in that violate moral principles. Brasnett explains:

> Of these pleasures God has a complete intellectual apprehension; he has, as it were, a scientific understanding of their nature and being, yet he has never felt them as his own, never made them his, never allowed them to penetrate to his inmost self, because they are evil, at least in part, and God's inmost self is wholly good.[227]

In positing that God has a complete intellectual apprehension of these creaturely emotional states, Brasnett seems to be saying that God fully grasps their evaluative judgments. Yet, Brasnett is denying that God has a grasp of the affect of these emotions because possessing the affect would be inconsistent with God's moral perfection. Brasnett affirms that God can have a grasp of the affect of a whole range of other emotions, just not any emotions that are immoral. It might be the case that Brasnett thinks God has no grasp of the affect of certain immoral emotions, although it is unclear from his writings. This option is available to a neoclassical theist if she wants it.

One might worry that this limits God's knowledge. The passibilist Francis McConnell is not deterred by such worries because he thinks that there are moral limits on God's knowledge in a way similar to how there are logical limits to God's knowledge. With logical limits to God's knowledge, God cannot know <I am Sally>. This is because God knows that He is not Sally. McConnell claims that something similar is going on with God's knowledge and morality. He writes:

> If the divine knowledge is based, so to speak, on sympathetic insight, does not such insight preclude a divine knowledge of evil? Of course it does, in any sympathetic experience. The divine God of the Christ knows more about some aspects of evil than any other intelligence. He knows more of its cost. Evil means more distress to him than anyone else. Still, he cannot know evil in the experience of friendly response to evil. He can have sympathy for the soul of low ideals, but not sympathy with that soul. If this is a limitation of the omniscience, let it be so. The approach to God through Christ is not concerned with the preservation of formal omniscience at the cost of moral worth.[228]

One could interpret McConnell as saying something like the following: there is a knowledge of what it is like to hate one's enemies, and God doesn't fully understand what that is like. God might have a fairly deep grasp of those

---

[227] (Brasnett 1928, 21).   [228] (McConnell 1927, 115).

phenomenal conscious states, but He does not have His own first-person perspective of what it is like to hate one's enemies. In other words, it seems like McConnell is denying that God has a perfect grasp of *all* conscious states in order to preserve God's moral perfection.

The passibilist Keith Ward makes a similar remark. He says:

> Still, though God's knowledge is perfect, we do not want to think of God actually feeling all the frustrations and sufferings that finite creatures undergo, just in the way that creatures do. Indeed, such a thing seems not to be possible, since part of creaturely suffering is sometimes the feeling that pain fills the whole of one's experience or that life itself is pointless and depressing. Further, many human experiences, for instance those of mass murderers, are intrinsically evil. Such experiences can never be experienced by God in that form. God must know that they occur and must know what they are like. But God will never actually experience that life is pointless, and God must condemn experiences that are intrinsically evil. So there must be a certain "distancing" of God from human experiences as we undergo them.[229]

Ward further comments:

> We must conclude that all human experiences will affect the divine experience and cause God to feel either empathy or condemnation, which would not exist in God without the occurrence of finite experiences. But human experiences as such cannot be the actual experiences of God.[230]

Ward's comments seem to suggest that this limitation on God's empathic knowledge is not simply due to inconsistency with God's moral perfection. There are also cases where certain phenomenal conscious states would be inconsistent with God's perfect rationality. As Ward explains: "God knows that we suffer and what it is like for us to suffer. But God also knows that our sufferings can in some way and at some time be subsumed within a greater whole in which we will find an overwhelming happiness."[231] Like Zagzebski, Ward maintains that God's empathy does not negate God's own perspective. When God empathizes with a creature, God does not lose sight of His own perspective, and what He knows. Hence, God will not always agree with the emotional judgment of the creature that He is empathizing with.

Consider an emotion like hopelessness. God can empathize with a creature who is feeling hopeless. God will feel the suffering of this creature, but it will not cause God to lose hope because God also knows His own master plan for creation. As Ward explains, God's empathetic knowledge is always associated with His own response of either condemnation or approval. As such, there will

---

[229] (Ward 2017, 174).   [230] (Ward 2017, 174).   [231] (Ward 2017, 174–5).

be gradations in God's experiential knowledge, and in the intensity of God's feelings.[232] In the case of hopelessness, God has some grasp of the intensity of the affect of hopelessness, but it does not cause God to have the emotion of hopelessness, neither does it cause God to feel utterly hopeless.

In response to the Problem of Mere Feeling, the neoclassical theist has a basic strategy for avoiding this problem. She can say that God has a perfect grasp of the evaluative judgments of creatures, but His grasp of the affects of creaturely emotions comes in varying degrees. In the case of immoral emotions, the intensity of the affect for God will be quite low, and perhaps nonexistent. In the case of emotions such as hopelessness, the intensity of the affect for God is higher, but not so high that God comes to experience hopelessness Himself. This, according to the neoclassical theist, is what maximal empathy looks like.

§6.3.1 An Objection to the Maximally Empathetic God

One might raise an objection to the maximal God option.

> OBJECTION: If the passibilist is denying that God can have a perfect grasp of all conscious states, why not deny all such phenomenal knowledge of God? It seems like the passibilist is undermining the argument for omnisubjectivity in her attempt to preserve God's moral perfection. If the arguments for omnisubjectivity are undermined, then some of the arguments against impassibility are undermined.

I think this objection is a bit hasty. The Maximal God thesis is saying that a morally perfect God cannot have certain kinds of phenomenal knowledge based on empathy. Thus, ruling out omnisubjectivity. However, the Maximal God thesis is still saying that God has maximal empathy. Nothing about moral perfection prevents God from having the maximally consistent degree of phenomenal knowledge based on empathy. A maximally empathetic God still has a broad range of emotional states and phenomenal knowledge that an impassible God cannot.

Passibilists such as McConnell and Brasnett can still argue that a morally perfect God must empathize with our suffering. There is nothing in empathetic suffering that violates the dictates of morality. Consider Thomas Aquinas' claim that the virtuous person is disturbed by witnessing certain acts of horror, or the moral sentimentalist claim that it is empathy that stirs us to right action. Empathy plays an important role in various ethical frameworks. In order to show that the Maximal God thesis undermines the case for passibilism, the classical theist will need to show that empathetic knowledge as a whole is

---

[232] (Ward 2017, 175).

inconsistent with moral perfection. That seems like a tall order. All that has been claimed in the Maximal God thesis is that certain instances of empathy are inconsistent with moral perfection. It has not been demonstrated that all cases of empathetic knowledge are inconsistent with moral perfection, and that is precisely what the classical theist needs to show in order to press the problem of divine empathy to such an extent that divine passibility is ruled out.

Conclusion

It is time to draw this Element to a close. Given the introductory nature of this Element, I do not consider myself to have offered a conclusive case for either impassibility or passibility. My goal has been to help the reader explore the different issues surrounding the debate over the emotional life of God. My hope is that I have offered more than enough food for thought that will help philosophers and theologians advance this debate in new and exciting ways. Will the twenty-first century see the comeback of divine impassibility? Or will the golden age of divine suffering continue? Perhaps the answer to these questions depends on how you, my dear reader, feel about the debate presented in this Element.

Bibliography

Aquinas, Thomas. 1993. *The Collected Works of St. Thomas Aquinas. Electronic Edition*, ed. John N. Deely. Charlottsville: InteLex Corporation.

Arminius, James. 1986. *The Works of James Arminius*. Trans. James Nichols. Vol. 2. London: Baker Book House Company.

Augustine, Saint. 1991. *The Trinity*. Trans. Edmund Hill. Hyde Park: New City Press.

Bates, William. 1999. *The Whole Works of the Rev. W. Bates*, ed. W. Farmer. Vol. 1. Harrisonburg: Sprinkle Publications.

Bauckham, Richard. 2008. *Jesus and the God of Israel: God Crucified and Other Studies on the New Testament's Christology of Divine Identity*. Grand Rapids: Wm. B. Eerdmans Publishing Co.

Bavinck, Herman. 1979. *The Doctrine of God*. Edinburgh: Banner of Truth Trust.

Bird, Michael F. 2013. *Evangelical Theology: A Biblical and Systematic Introduction*. Grand Rapids: Zondervan.

Blackwood, Christopher. 1658. *Expositions and Sermons Upon the Ten First Chapters of the Gospel of Jesus Christ, According to Matthew*. London: Henry Hills.

Brady, Michael S. 2013. *Emotional Insight: The Epistemic Role of Emotional Experience*. Oxford: Oxford University Press.

Brasnett, Bertrand R. 1928. *The Suffering of the Impassible God*. London: Macmillan.

Carson, D.A. 2006. *How Long, O Lord? Reflections on Suffering and Evil*. Grand Rapids: Baker Academic.

Carson, D.A. 2000. "Love." In *New Dictionary of Biblical Theology*, eds. T. Desmond Alexander, Brian S. Rosner, D.A. Carson, and Graeme Goldsworthy. Downers Grove: InterVarsity Press.

Charnock, Stephen. 1864. *The Complete Works of Stephen Charnock*. ed. James M'Cosh. Vol. 1. Edinburgh: James Nichol.

Clore, Gerald L. 2011. "Psychology and the Rationality of Emotion." *Modern Theology* 27: 325–38.

Craig, William Lane. 2001. *God, Time, and Eternity: The Coherence of Theism II: Eternity*. London: Kluwer Academic Publishers.

Creel, Richard E. 1997. "Immutability and Impassibility." In *A Companion to Philosophy of Religion*, eds. Philip L. Quinn and Charles Taliaferro. Malden: Blackwell Publishing.

Creel, Richard E. 1986. *Divine Impassibility: An Essay in Philosophical Theology*. Cambridge: Cambridge University Press.

Cuneo, Terence. 2007. *The Normative Web: An Argument for Moral Realism*. Oxford: Oxford University Press.

Davies, Brian. 2006. *The Reality of God and the Problem of Evil*. London: Continuum International Publishing Group.

Davies, Brian and G.R. Evans,. 2008. *Anselm of Canterbury: The Major Works*. New York: Oxford University.

Deng, Natalja. 2018. *God and Time*. Cambridge: Cambridge University Press.

Deonna, Julien A. and Fabrice Teroni. 2012. *The Emotions: A Philosophical Introduction*. New York: Routledge.

Diller, Jeanine and Asa Kasher. 2013. *Models of God and Alternative Ultimate Realities*. New York: Springer.

Dodds, Michael J. 2008. *The Unchanging God of Love: Thomas Aquinas and Contemporary Theology on Divine Immutability*. 2nd ed. Washington DC: Catholic University of America Press.

Dolezal, James E. 2019. "Strong Impassibility." In *Divine Impassibility: Four Views of God's Emotions and Suffering*, eds. Robert J. Matz and A. Chadwick Thornhill. Downers Grove: IVP Academic.

Dolezal, James E. 2017. *All That Is In God: Evangelical Theology and the Challenge of Classical Christian Theism*. Grand Rapids: Reformation Heritage Books.

Fiddes, Paul. 1988. *The Creative Suffering of God*. Oxford: Oxford University Press.

Fretheim, Terence E. 1984. *The Suffering of God: An Old Testament Perspective*. Philadelphia: Fortress Press.

Gallagher, Shaun. 2017. "Empathy and Theories of Direct Perception." In *The Routledge Handbook of Philosophy of Empathy*, ed. Heidi L. Maibom. London: Routledge.

Gavrilyuk, Paul L. 2004. *The Suffering of the Impassible God: The Dialectics of Patristic Thought*. Oxford: Oxford University Press.

Hartshorne, Charles. 1964. *Man's Vision of God and the Logic of Theism*. Hamden: Archon Books.

Hasker, William. 2016. "Is Divine Simplicity a Mistake?" *American Catholic Philosophical Quarterly* 90: 600–725.

Heil, John. 2018. "Dispositionality and Mentality." In *The Ontology of Emotions*, eds. Hichem Naar and Fabrice Teroni. Cambridge: Cambridge University Press.

Helm, Bennett W. 2015. "Emotions and Recalcitrance: Reevaluating the Perceptual Model." *Dialectica* 2015: 417–33.

Helm, Bennett W. 2001. "Emotions and Practical Reason: Rethinking Evaluation and Motivation." *Nous* 35.

Helm, Paul. 2014. "Impassionedness and 'So-called Classical Theism'." In *Within the Love of God: Essays on the Doctrine of God in Honour of Paul S. Fiddes*, eds. Anthony Clarke and Andrew Moore. Oxford: Oxford University Press.

Helm, Paul. 2010. *Eternal God: A Study of God Without Time*. 2nd ed. Oxford: Oxford University Press.

Helm, Paul. 1990. "Impossibility of Divine Passibility." In *The Power and Weakness of God*, ed. Nigel M. de S. Cameron. Edinburgh: Rutherford House Books.

Herdt, Jennifer A. 2001. "The Rise of Sympathy and the Question of Divine Suffering." *Journal of Religious Ethics* 29: 367–99.

Kauppinen, Antti. 2017. "Empathy and Moral Judgment." In *The Routledge Handbook of Philosophy of Empathy*, ed. Heidi L. Maibom. London: Routledge.

Kennett, Jeanette. 2017. "Empathy and Psychopathology." In *The Routledge Handbook of Philosophy of Empathy*, ed. Heidi L. Maibom. London: Routledge.

Kraay, Klaas J. 2010. "Theism, Possible Worlds, and the Multiverse." *Philosophical Studies* 147: 355–68.

Lane, Tony. 2001. "The Wrath of God as an Aspect of the Love of God." In *Nothing Greater, Nothing Better: Theological Essays on the Love of God*, ed. Kevin J. Vanhoozer.Grand Rapids: William B. Eerdmans Publishing Company.

Lindberg, Carter. 2008. *Love: A Brief History Through Western Christianity*. Oxford: Blackwell Publishing.

Lister, Rob. 2013. *God is Impassible and Impassioned: Toward a Theology of Divine Emotion*. Wheaton: Crossway.

Lombard, Peter. 2007. *The Sentences Book 1: The Mystery of the Trinity*. Trans. Giulio Silano. Ontario: Pontifical Institute of Mediaeval Studies.

Maibom, Heidi L. 2017. "Affective Empathy." In *The Routledge Handbook of Philosophy of Empathy*, ed. Heidi L. Maibom. London: Routledge.

Mawson, T.J. 2018. *The Divine Attributes*. Cambridge: Cambridge University Press.

Mawson, T.J. 2008. "Divine Eternity." *International Journal for the Philosophy of Religion* 64: 35–50.

McConnell, Francis J. 1927. *The Christlike God: A Survey of the Divine Attributes From the Christian Point of View*. New York: Abingdon Press.

McConnell, Francis J. 1924. *Is God Limited?* London: Williams & Norgate.

Moberly, R.W.L. 2013. *Old Testament Theology: Reading the Hebrew Bible as Christian Scripture*. Grand Rapids: Baker Academic.

Moberly, R.W.L. 1998. "God is Not a Human That He Should Repent (Numbers 23:19 and 1 Samuel 15:29)." In *God in the Fray: A Tribute to Walter Brueggemann*, eds. Tod Linafelt and Timothy K. Beal. Minneapolis: Fortress Press.

Moltmann, Jurgen. 2001. *The Crucified God: The Cross of Christ as the Foundation and Criticism of Christian Theology*. London: SCM.

Mozley, J.K. 1926. *The Impassibility of God: A Survey of Christian Thought*. Cambridge: Cambridge University Press.

Muis, Jan. 2011. "Can Christian Talk About God Be Literal?" *Modern Theology* 27: 582–607.

Mullins, R.T. 2018. "Why Can't the Impassible God Suffer?" *TheoLogica* 2: 3–22.

Mullins, R.T. 2016a. *The End of the Timeless God*. Oxford: Oxford University Press.

Mullins, R.T. 2016b. "The Difficulty of Demarcating Panentheism." *Sophia* 55: 325–46.

Mullins, R.T. 2014. "Doing Hard Time: Is God the Prisoner of the Oldest Dimension?" *Journal of Analytic Theology* 2: 160–85.

Nagasawa, Yujin. 2017. *Maximal God: A New Defense of Perfect Being Theism*. Oxford : Oxford University Press.

Nagasawa, Yujin. 2013. "Models of Anselmian Theism." *Faith and Philosophy* 30: 3–25.

Nagasawa, Yujin. 2008. *God and Phenomenal Consciousness: A Novel Approach to Knowledge Arguments*. Cambridge: Cambridge University Press.

Nagasawa, Yujin. 2003. "Divine Omniscience and Knowledge *de se*." *International Journal for Philosophy of Religion* 53: 73–82.

Nussbaum, Martha C. 2001. *Upheavals of Thought: Intelligence of Emotions*. Cambridge: Cambridge University Press.

O'Connor, Kathleen M. 1998. "The Tears of God and Divine Character in Jeremiah 2–9." In *God in the Fray: A Tribute to Walter Brueggemann*, eds. Tod Linafelt and Timothy K. Beal. Minneapolis: Fortress Press.

Oord, Thomas Jay. 2019. *God Can't!* New York City: SacraSage Press.

Oord, Thomas Jay. 2010. *The Nature of Love: A Theology*. St Louis: Chalice Press.

Peckham, John C. 2019. "Qualified Passibility." In *Divine Impassibility: Four Views of God's Emotions and Suffering*, eds. Robert J. Matz and A. Chadwick Thornhill. Downers Grove: IVP Academic.

Peckham, John C. 2015. *The Love of God: A Canonical Model*. Downers Grove: IVP Academic.

Pereboom, Derk. 2016. "Libertarianism and Theological Determinism." In *Free Will and Theism: Connections, Contingencies, and Concerns*, eds. Kevin Timpe and Daniel Speak. Oxford: Oxford University Press.

Pink, Arthur W. 1975. *The Attributes of God*. Grand Rapids: Baker Books.

Randles, Marshall. 1900. *The Blessed God: Impassibility*. London: Charles H. Kelly.

Ravenscroft, Ian. 2017. "Empathy and Knowing What It's Like." In *The Routledge Handbook of Philosophy of Empathy*, ed. Heidi L. Maibom. London: Routledge.

Renihan, Samuel, ed. 2015. *God Without Passions: A Reader*. Palmdale: Reformed Baptist Academic Press.

Rice, Rebekah L. 2016. "Reasons and Divine Action." In *Free Will and Theism: Connections, Contingencies, and Concerns*, eds. Kevin Timpe and Daniel Speak. Oxford: Oxford University Press.

Roberts, Robert C. 2013. *Emotions in the Moral Life*. Cambridge: Cambridge University Press.

Roberts, Robert C. 2011. *Thinking Through Feeling: God, Emotion and Passibility*. New York: Continuum International Publishing Group.

Roberts, Robert C. 2007. *Spiritual Emotions: A Psychology of Christian Virtues*. Grand Rapids: William B. Eerdmans Publishing Company.

Roberts, Robert C. and W. Jay Wood. 2007. *Intellectual Virtues: An Essay in Regulative Epistemology*. New York: Oxford University Press.

Rogers, Katherin. 1996. "The Traditional Doctrine of Divine Simplicity." *Religious Studies* 32.

Scrutton, Anastasia. 2013. "Divine Passibility: God and Emotion." *Philosophy Compass* 8: 866–74.

Shafer-Landau, Russ. 2005. *Moral Realism: A Defence*. Oxford: Oxford University Press.

Shedd, W.G.T. 1888. *Dogmatic Theology*. Vol. 1. New York: Charles Scribner's Sons.

Shoemaker, David. 2017. "Empathy and Moral Responsibility." In *The Routledge Handbook of Philosophy of Empathy*, ed. Heidi L. Maibom. London: Routledge.

Silverman, Eric. 2013. "Impassibility and Divine Love." In *Models of God and Alternative Ultimate Realities*, eds. Jeanine Diller and Asa Kasher. New York: Springer.

Soteriou, Matthew. 2018. "The Ontology of Emotion." In *The Ontology of Emotions*, eds. Hichem Naar and Fabrice Teroni. Cambridge: Cambridge University Press.

Spaulding, Shannon. 2017. "Cognitive Empathy." In *The Routledge Handbook of Philosophy of Empathy*, ed. Heidi L. Maibom. London: Routledge.

Strong, Augustus Hopkins. 1907a. *Systematic Theology Volume 1: The Doctrine of God*. Philadelphia: American Baptist Publication Society.

Strong, Augustus Hopkins. 1907b. *Systematic Theology Volume 2: The Doctrine of Man*. Philadelphia: American Baptist Publication Society.

Stump, Eleonore. 2018. *Atonement*. Oxford: Oxford University Press.

Stump, Eleonore. 2010. *Wandering in Darkness: Narrative and the Problem of Suffering*. Oxford: Oxford University Press.

Swinburne, Richard. 2016. *The Coherence of Theism*. Oxford: Oxford University Press.

Ta, Vivian P. and William Ickes. 2017. "Empathic Accuracy." In *The Routledge Handbook of Philosophy of Empathy*, ed. Heidi L. Maibom. London: Routledge.

Taliaferro, Charles. 1989. "The Possibility of God." *Religious Studies* 25: 217–24.

Timpe, Kevin. 2013. "Introduction to Neo-Classical Theism." In *Models of God and Alternative Ultimate Realities*, eds. Jeanine Diller and Asa Kasher. New York: Springer.

Todd, Cain. 2014. "Emotion and Value." *Philosophy Compass* 9: 702–12.

Ussher, James. 1645. *A Body of Divinitie, or the Summe and Substance of Christian Religion*. London: M.F.

Wainwright, William J. 2016. *Reason, Revelation, and Devotion: Inference and Argument in Religion*. Cambridge: Cambridge University Press.

Ward, Keith. 2017. *The Christian Idea of God: A Philosophical Foundation for Faith*. Cambridge: Cambridge University Press.

Wessel, Susan. 2016. *Passion and Compassion in Early Christianity*. Cambridge: Cambridge University Press.

Wittmann, Tyler. 2016. "The Logic of Divine Blessedness and the Salvific Teleology of Christ." *International Journal of Systematic Theology* 18.

Wolterstorff, Nicholas. 2010. *Inquiring About God*, ed. Terence Cuneo. Cambridge: Cambridge University Press.

Zagzebski, Linda. 2016. "Omnisubjectivity: Why It Is a Divine Attribute." *Nova et Vetera* 14: 435–50.

Zagzebski, Linda. 2013. *Omnisubjectivity: A Defense of a Divine Attribute*. Milwaukee: Marquette University Press.

Zagzebski, Linda. 2008. "Omnisubjectivity." In *Oxford Studies in Philosophy of Religion*, ed. Jonathan L. Kvanvig. New York: Oxford University Press.

Zahavi, Dan. 2017. "Phenomenology, Empathy, and Mindreading." In *The Routledge Handbook of Philosophy of Empathy*, ed. Heidi L. Maibom. London: Routledge.

Zanchius, Girolamo. 1601. *Life Everlasting: Or, The True Knowledge of One Jehovah, Three Elohim, and Jesus Immanuel.* Cambridge: John Legat.

Acknowledgments

Many thanks to various individuals for continued discussion on the topic of this book. In particular, Lara Casewell, Ruth Lyons, Lins McRobie, and Ema Sani. Special thanks to Chantal Incandela and Liz Ladd for helping me understand the difference between emotional contagion and empathy. Much gratitude towards Kimberley Kroll, Jeremy Rios, and Taylor Telford for helping me narrow the focus of the book. Deep appreciation for those who read earlier drafts of this material, and offered feedback: James Arcadi, Colby Brandt, Xanthe Davison, Thomas Kane, Thomas Jay Oord, John Peckham, Hazel Quemi, Tasia Scrutton, Jordan Selfe, JT Turner, Barnaby Webster, and Jordan Wessling.

Cambridge Elements ≡

Philosophy of Religion

Yujin Nagasawa

University of Birmingham

Yujin Nagasawa is Professor of Philosophy and Co-Director of the John Hick Centre for Philosophy of Religion at the University of Birmingham. He is currently President of the British Society for the Philosophy of Religion. He is a member of the Editorial Board of *Religious Studies*, the *International Journal for Philosophy of Religion* and *Philosophy Compass*.

About the Series

This Cambridge Elements series provides concise and structured introductions to all the central topics in the philosophy of religion. It offers balanced, comprehensive coverage of multiple perspectives in the philosophy of religion. Contributors to the series are cutting-edge researchers who approach central issues in the philosophy of religion. Each provides a reliable resource for academic readers and develops new ideas and arguments from a unique viewpoint.

Cambridge Elements ☰

Philosophy of Religion

Elements in the Series

The Design Argument
Elliott Sober

God and Time
Natalja Deng

Continental Philosophy of Religion
Elizabeth Burns

Religious Diversity and Religious Progress
Robert McKim

Religious Fictionalism
Robin Le Poidevin

God and Morality
Anne Jeffrey

God, Soul and the Meaning of Life
Thaddeus Metz

God and Human Freedom
Leigh C. Vicens and Simon Kittle

God and Abstract Objects
Einar Duenger Bøhn

The Problem of Evil
Michael Tooley

God and Emotion
R. T. Mullins

A full series listing is available at: www.cambridge.org/EPREL

Printed in the United States
By Bookmasters